globalized Wisdom of the XXI Century

Federico Sulimovich

Treatises & Essays

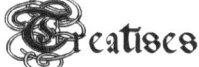

Globalized Wisdom of the XXI Century

3rd Edition

© 2013 Federico Sulimovich
All Rights Reserve
ISBN 978-0-615-91135-9

dedicated to

*This book
is a sort of summary of the main ideas
of main world religions and philosophies
organized and explained
following a purely logic structure
which seeks to unify them.*

index

chapter	page
introduction	7
Originally only one	13
The logic of the mystic	17
The elements, and their mutations	39
The experience	75
Love, passion and commitment	79
Beggar, king, and sage	83
Father, mother and son	89
Journal of impressions	93
bibliography	129

— for beginners only —

introduction

All struggles arise because each person seeks to impose their own point of view. We tell ourselves that our purpose is the truly true, and that blessings will come to all alike if we abide by the rules and perform the rituals—if we take up the means, and carry out the sacred steps that lead us toward fulfillment. We speak of happiness in words arranged like incantations; but when words fail, we turn to force. It would seem that fulfillment is different for everyone, that each carries their own, and that both creation and destruction could grant it to us in equal measure, depending on the situation.

We also observe that we all feel satisfied by a meal earned through effort; it would seem that satisfaction, too, dwells where it delights in watching us strive and work. We arrive in this world from we know not where, as if drawn forth by a breath older than time—urged by a hidden flame to eat, to labor, to love, to die. And yet within us stir sensations like winds through tall grass, thoughts that flicker like starlight on water, and visions that rise like flame—drawing us toward something vast and luminous beyond ourselves. Let us call these ideas spirits. In this vision, God created the world so that these spirits—each a maker of its own realm—could coexist. Humanity was meant to judge these ideas and give them form through action. But in losing God, man becomes ensnared by the very spirits he was meant to guide.

Every action owes itself to its result. So then—what is the action that leads to happiness? To act upon this or that idea? To resist it, or try to manage the desires of others? Those who follow their desires and succeed often find that it is not enough. Their reward fades. They return to the same road, again and again, thinking that a more perfect effort will finally satisfy. But happiness leaves behind only its trace. Time moves on, and all that remains is the memory. If we tie happiness to objects of desire, it will vanish as quickly as it appears.

Some see this and choose to step away from desire. But even renunciation becomes a pursuit. They hope that by constantly letting go, something deeper will emerge—like a hidden spring beneath dry earth, waiting to rise through stillness and silence. Others move toward or away from desire, aware that what is desired is not what brings or holds the joy. And in doing so, they free happiness from the weight of results. They are said to have overcome desire because they carry within them a quiet abundance, capable of blooming in any moment—not just the one they once longed for. They seek nothing to claim, and reject nothing that comes. They move with life as it is. It is like the difference between a child and an adult before a sweet treat—the child weeps when denied; the adult lets it pass.

Happiness may be reached by fulfilling desire, surrendering it, or transcending it through something higher. The right path depends on the moment, but one of these three always applies. On the other hand, if one seeks peace with oneself, a single act of genuine giving may suffice—so long as we do not later demand something in return.

The search for fulfillment is what every ritual symbolizes; yet in truth, the ritual is not performed to obtain it, but because it is what fulfillment itself once delighted in doing through us. In the East, people ended their labors by gathering to drink tea, and so tea became a ceremony of peace. The Christians did likewise with bread. Though happiness wears many masks, it carries the same essence—a fullness that flows through each and ties them together in one holy spirit.

This shared fullness, moving freely through all things, is the final longing behind every search—like a fragrance that travels unseen, or a light resting softly on water. Though appearances suggest each person has their own happiness, it is always the same fullness, seen from different angles. It does not come through effort—it arrives on its own, like a bird alighting on an open hand, when we no longer grasp, when we leave space for it to land. In its presence, no desire remains to be pursued, for we are already content with what is, wherever we are.

This joy that lives in union with all can be known beneath any sky, within any skin—felt in the hush of shared silence, in the warmth of a held hand, or in the quiet grace of morning light falling across a table. And yet, we tend to return to the places and moments where it once touched us, believing we might find it there again. In doing so, we shape rituals—repeating gestures, settings, and movements that once made us whole—hoping they might summon it back. Desire reveals itself as a sign of something missing, and a path we feel must be followed. But in truth, it speaks more like a premonition than a command. If we hear it as such, we need not chase so desperately—we may simply wait, and let what is meant for us arrive.

And if what we hoped for finally arrives but leaves us hollow, it is because we discover too late that it carried no light of its own. In every gain, something is lost. Every goal takes something from us. We often grieve what we gave up more than we celebrate what was won. If we were given sudden wealth or power, our old selves—habits, routines, small pleasures—would fade. Even if we tried to keep both, we would know it was never the same.

Gain and loss walk side by side. Becoming something new requires leaving something behind. But we do not always see this. We put too much faith in the promise of gain. If we won the lottery, we might say, "Everything is now perfect." But that belief brings new trouble, crafted in the image of our wish. The wise knew this: that loss must come first, through chosen sacrifice, before true gain can root. First duty, then desire. First effort, then reward.

No gain is absolute. Still, we tire of the effort. We long for something always ready, always whole. Is that wrong? No—it is natural. Our longing for perfect happiness is as natural as the plant bending toward the sun. Along our way, we gather dreams, plans, bright moments. These are not the thing itself, only flickers of it.

Nothing we do can grant us perfect joy, for all our actions are limited, and the world is finite. True happiness—like love, like the divine—cannot be earned. Still, we would give up all passing beauty for even one glimpse. Beneath every act is this single yearning. But we cannot force it, cannot shape it. We cannot stop desiring it, and yet cannot make it real.

We cry, sometimes silently, "Please—let me out."

When we see our efforts lead nowhere—that they are distractions, and no longer even bring us joy—we are left with a choice. We can continue in quiet despair, or surrender to the first thing that promises peace, even if it is hollow. Without knowing what we seek, we are easily led astray.

We cannot become whole through doing. Every act changes us, and each change costs something. Even if we become the wisest or most powerful, we will always find something we do not want. And in that resistance, we remain split. Fullness cannot be forced or divided into results. Even science, the deeper it goes, the more it sees how little it knows. Every answer opens a new question. And yet we keep searching. And so, though the search does not create happiness, it does unfold a richness of scenery—expanding the ground where joy might choose to appear.

In the end, if no means and no goal can offer us true fulfillment, it may be because we are meant to become what we have always been: that boundless fullness which, in imagining itself as a goal, enclosed itself within its own longing. We feel terribly unhappy, and there seems to be nothing we can do to mend it. Yet reason, the voice of the divine, and the quiet evidence of lived experience all point to the same truth: that fulfillment already breathes within us, quiet and unchanged.

God murmurs that it dwells in the heart of all things. Reason reminds us that the subject can never be reduced to an object. And our experiences, like mirrors held over time, eventually reflect it back to us. If I do not feel this truth, it is because I have turned against myself. Desire draws the soul inward, folding it into the body, where it suffers the narrowness of its own longing. Behind every end, behind every purpose, what we truly seek is only what we already are—a cosmos of possibility.

When sadness appears, happiness becomes no more than a memory—of a time when it burned more brightly. It lingers like an impression I cannot shake, like an echo reverberating through the mind. But if instead of granting happiness to those echoes of the past, I place it in my present disposition, then my attention becomes its only condition. And I no longer have reason to name what is happening to me as unhappiness, insufficiency, or loss. Whatever change I undergo, I remain utterly captivated by the purity of creation, and quietly astonished by its movements.

Thus, the way to fullness is not to do fullness, but to be it. For there can be no method to attain what was never meant to be a goal. Fullness finds us—it arrives when it wills, and most of all, when we make space for it. If we act in pursuit of it, we may indeed find a result—but once that result fades, so too will our sense of wholeness. And so we repeat the same actions, believing fullness to be nothing more than their fleeting echo.

But if I am already that fullness, I must confront the false longing or pain that veils it, and turn instead to witness the change unfolding before me. To meet that change with open awareness is to dissolve its sharpness. With truth as our companion, we can face what is difficult, painful, or tangled—and allow it, through clarity, to become the root of transformation.

If, on the other hand, we conclude that happiness does not exist, then suffering too must vanish—for suffering is nothing but the hunger for joy. And if even suffering falls away, what remains is pure existence, vast and unbounded. We cannot expect all of life—even in its fullness—to be pleasurable. Pleasure belongs to the self we've constructed; it has little to do with truth. Sweet and bitter are but two faces of the same coin.

When we fear the difficult, and retreat from the work and weight of responsibility, life begins to harden. What we avoid becomes the burden. What we postpone becomes the crisis. We prefer the easy, we put off the effort, we choose delight first—yet in doing so, we only feed the storm we fear. But when we face the unpleasant first, we often find it was not pain at all, but only the shadow of our hesitation. And even in error, we learn. Even in discomfort, we grow.

Through effort, we pass into peace. And looking back, we find there was no suffering after all—only moments that asked us to walk through the unknown. The longer we delay, the darker those moments become. All this, because we cling to relative pleasure—pleasure that must be fed and guarded, that demands effort we would rather avoid.

And yet, in spite of everything, happiness finds its way. Even when we say it doesn't exist, it appears. Even when denied, it finds a crack to shine through—quiet, luminous, and impossible to escape.

— base of the treatises —

Originally only One

It divided itself in two,
turning toward itself,
creating the mirror to behold itself;
to touch,
to smell,
to taste,
to hear,
to feel,
to think,
to darken,
to shine,
to dance its endless dance,
and to lose itself in play, just to rediscover itself again.

The One gazes upon itself.
And in this encounter, space arises,
giving way to relief, contour, folds of creation.
A distance appears between itself and itself,
but this distance is only apparent:
an illusion, a form it willingly takes on.
So in every shape, in every curve of being,
it is always there.

It steps outside itself to return to itself,
spinning, generating movement;
and in that movement, it creates moments of itself.

Like a dancer shifting through postures,
from stillness into motion,
and from motion back to stillness.

Thus arises the imagined difference
between form and essence,
between "I" and "That,"
the seer and the seen.

And so the One flows through you and through me.
Because we are the One,
we imitate it,
dividing ourselves within as it once did;
creating and confronting sensation and thought,
action and result, dream and reality,
past, present, and future,
success and failure.
All forms and appearances are woven this way,
from the simplest to the most complex.

The One knows both forms are itself,
and so there is no conflict.
To see that you and I are the same being,
even as we appear utterly different brings completion.
But to make creation more playful,
its forms plunge into the forgetfulness of their own origin,
so they may rediscover themselves
through time and experience.
Everything is prepared for this.

One who does not see themselves as the One
divides life into two: Me and Not-Me, the world.
Within both, what is born and what dies.
When we cling to what is born, we feel joy.
When we cling to what dies, we feel sorrow.
This is the common habit of this world.
And what is born or dies can be anything:
a person, an object, an idea, a project, a feeling.

So you and I adopt the four basic stances
and spin around them:

—I feel sorrow and think of myself:
    (I must be wrong, I don't know how I can be like this;
    I need to change.)

—I feel sorrow and think of the world:
    (I blame the world for my pain;
    I long to set things right.)

—I feel joy and think of myself:
    (Nothing is better than me,
    the source of joy itself.)

—I feel joy and think of the world:
    (Fully absorbed,
    passionately entangled.)

It makes no difference which one we favor; one cannot exist without the other. Birth and death merge, knowledge and ignorance give rise to one another. It is you and I taking turns, inhabiting each face, each gesture.

So I move through these four positions, rejecting the other three as outside me, and seeing them play out across the world. Our divided selves orbit these stances, clinging to one, resisting its opposite, day after day, life after life.

There are two ways to transcend this: either the self renounces all identification—denying all affirmation; or the self embraces the opposite within—affirming every negation.

Thus, in the act of confronting or embracing one another, we begin to see that both are held within a third voice: the Word, as it was in the beginning. And the three of us—self, other, and the Word—move gently from one to the next, blending with and within the movement itself, entering a state of ever-renewing, dreamlike dimensions. You can be the person you wish to be, the god you long to become, or simply what is.

- treatise 1 -

The logic of the mystic

Something must be done. It cannot be that our desires go unfulfilled, especially when they reach toward something so vast, so immeasurable. I wrestle with a suffering I myself keep alive, feeding it with constant attention, making it more elusive, more unsolvable.

It seems a new thought has surfaced...

It seems that whenever I trail off into silence, that is when I feel—and from that feeling, thought begins to rise. Like those moments of learning, when a realization bursts forth and we exclaim: "Eureka!" Then knowledge arises—of what was felt, and of what was seen.

Can I use that knowledge for anything?

And so my thoughts multiply, and with them, life becomes more complicated. Thankfully, that ringing in my head fades when I truly face those thoughts—though it often returns, cloaked in a comment, a doubt, a whisper.

In moments of joy, of fullness, thought seems silent—simply witnessing. That presence... which, when it loses its purity or unity, begins to think about what it once touched: beatitude, and being.

Most of the time, we find ourselves circling good and evil, searching for the end of the search itself, wondering why we cannot simply reach for what we desire. But the truth is—we can. Only if we are willing to pay the price.

And why must everything that flows in this vast universe come with a price?

The universe arranges its wonders in the most absurd ways. If I don't even know what I am... how could I possibly know about prices? Much less laws of the universe?

Life is a constant interaction with that nature always present, emerging from the unknown.

Thought performs a function of discrimination. It compares what is known—its stored memory, the portion of being it has claimed as its own (thesis)—with the new, the yet-unknown that now arises (antithesis). Based on experience, it weighs them, either adopting the new or clinging to the familiar. In that interplay, something shifts: a synthesis forms, bringing change—a direction we might follow or not, always leaving something behind. Thus, thought trims and molds what it can salvage from those precious, magical flashes we call happiness.

The artist of life moves back and forth, giving and receiving, accepting and refusing. It associates by dissociating and dissociates by associating. All it truly can do is affirm or deny what has already been experienced, filtering one into another. And when it no longer filters—when it pauses—it makes way for feeling.

Feeling is vibration, a pulse that, like thought, comes and goes in varied intensities—expanded or condensed, pleasant or painful, drawn or repelled. It gives texture to distance, shape to form, substance to all that surrounds us: matter itself. But even matter is only light and darkness dancing back and forth, holding within them a rainbow that calls to me—so I go to see...

And I realize: each time I say "yes" to one thing, I am at once saying "no" to another—two sides of the same impulse, equally real, moving in opposite directions. To move toward something is already to push something else away. Whenever I move forward, something is left behind. And when too much emphasis is placed on one of the poles, the opposite is stirred into motion—what seemed left behind will, sooner or later, appear again ahead.

Only through the meeting and reconciliation between opposites—between fantasy and reality—do meaningful images arise. Being is born from this union. It may emerge in matter or imagination, in object or subject. In youth, God is a fantasy full of meaning, a dream we try to shape. But in time, this fantasy becomes more real than reality—for one day, what we held as real will dissolve.

This is why to be realistic and objective is, in the end, impossible. Matter is nothing without the subject—without me. Whether I am pure fantasy and the world is real, or I am the truth and the world illusion, becomes only like a matter of philosophical preference.

Reality is to fantasy as husband is to wife, thought to feeling, subject to object, light to darkness. A dance of opposites, all angles of one whole—seen from the eyes of the One who is everything and nothing. If God is All, then God is light and also shadow. Thus, in His freedom, He permits us to stray so far we no longer see or hear Him. And in this distance were born the planetary shadows and forms—beings who wandered too far, and now plead not to be left in suffering.

If one can gaze both at what comes and what goes, and see that both are ever-changing, then one transcends. And in that eternal shifting, one is lifted into the current of the Word—that which holds both motion and stillness, and never dies. Yet by nature, we fix our gaze in only one direction.

By the riverbank, watching water endlessly arrive and depart, we wonder: Where does it come from? Where does it go? If I were to follow the current, I would see there is no beginning, no end—no true coming, no true going—only transformation. Cyclical by nature, it spins upon itself.

Its origin and destination appear only from where we stand. Fire and water meet in life, and together they carry us into the current— to that very moment when they touch and burst into thunders of gifts. Thus, following the cycle, as clouds, the dead in dreams rise upward, they gather, they swell, they condense in the sky— and when they are full, they fall once more into action.

We turn to light by instinct and abandon the dark. But once we're filled with light, we long for its opposite. Often, we try to light the darkness with our newfound brilliance, to fix the black hole with our little torch. Inevitably, we exhaust ourselves and retreat into the deepest shadows—until, having become darkness itself, we pass through it, and awaken. Then, we must head back toward the light we left behind, risking the path and its confusions, feeling the disappointment that darkness did not follow us. And so, we turn again—and again.

And all this deepens each time, in the glory of happiness, we take something for ourselves—because even if we take only life from the spark, we must die to return it. And all things will return, demanding back the light we clenched in our fist, responding according to what we once offered when we seized the bounty of the gift.

All glory ends. And when we look ahead once more, we face the unthinkable, the unknown—a void that feels senseless. Because in staring too long at what we love, we lose sight of what comes next. And that, we name ignorance, suffering, labor, duty.

It would be wiser to let the good pass by—ungrasped, uninflated, unbound. Let the current carry it, and turn our gaze to what's coming, not what has gone. For it is the looking back that wounds us. The more we cling, the more painful the letting go.

But if we attend to the unknown, to what we resist—the effort, the work, the heavy path—then once we set out, we will again see goodness approaching.

Only if we are insecure or possessive do we cling to moments of glory and recoil from the vast, terrifying void. We try to hide it, fill it, alter it, deny it—anything but look at it. Yet this is the very path we must walk, to reach the place where fire and water, this earth of sensation and this sky of possibility, once met, parted, turned, beheld each other... and reunited in God's spark.

Our desires are orders to God. In the blood of man, a new current rises. Life opens to us, so that we may fulfill ourselves and harvest the sacrifice of what was. Thus we are pointed toward what comes next. And by the Word we choose—spoken or silent—life turns once more.

Any aspiration—be it knowledge, peace, pleasure, holiness, art, money, science, transcendence, spirit, or anything else—is still a form of seeking. And every realization demands a sacrifice... and conceals a blind spot. To attain it, we must let go of it, and begin the work. To master any art, we begin with countless tedious exercises that render us incapable of attending to anything else. The wise one is first the one who does not know—thus, they learn. And when they learn, they realize all they still do not know.

For it to be day on the planet of pleasure, we must first charge ourselves with energy during its night. To reach the object of our love, we must first choose to set aside our fanciful desires—and instead, serve its source, its need, its inner divinity. The object of love is granted to the one who postpones themselves—who remains rational, objective, and clear in their seeing. That is why they are loved.

This is the meaning spoken by the master of the diamond, behind that famed sentence, the one that eternally undoes itself: "What is... is not—and so it is said to be." Its power lies in halting our speech and placing us firmly where we stand—even if our standing occurs only because we cannot move. We must remember what reality we began from... or whether we ever began at all.

If we observe ourselves closely, we see how we move from affirmation to negation through many cycles. In a single day, our thoughts deny and affirm countless times. Our mood swings from one side to the other. Even the brain reveals these waves:

in an active, calculating mind, oscillating between affirming and negating, the rhythm is about 14 cycles per second—Beta state. In a relaxed, contemplative mind: 8 to 13—Alpha. As sleep approaches: 4 to 7—Theta. And during sleep: a gentle ½ to 6—Delta. So we have daily cycles of affirmation and negation. Monthly, yearly, even great epochal cycles. And all of them function in the same way. We are, in a sense, a great chain of contradictions.

For every minimal affirmation or denial, there exists another—larger and more encompassing. And another after that. Until we finally ask: what do I truly want when I say no? What do I truly want when I say yes? We try to forge absolute yeses and absolute nos. But what really happens when I say yes is that something—or someone—appears to say no, with equal force, simply waiting for their moment. And if I say no, yes will return to chase me. All because of the Word at play. Though opposite in nature, these two forces share something essential—a common root that unites and divides them so that they might unfold. Every grave conflict begins with the desire to possess that which both holds us and separates us. We discriminate on the basis of a first shared trait—something that binds us even in division. Thus, the threefold reality is everywhere present: first, second, and third person. The Word. You. And I.

We could even draw a mathematical graph—a diagram of just this rigid pattern of three dimensions, generated by each Word, that makes up human life. One curve represents the conscious, expressed through thought, feeling, or matter—of me, of you, or of them. It depends on where our awareness resides in that moment. Another curve mirrors it in the unknown unconscious of our being.

And between the two, a third—though truly the first. The golden thread that connects and holds them both. This is the Word. This is happiness. This is God.

Thought, feeling, and the world—each rotates through three

states: positive, negative, and neutral. Happiness tends to sit in the middle, untouched, as the good and the bad revolve around it. The unity of God has been poured out—a self-offering that lets all things circle around it. And joy—impatient, eager—rushes to pin the medal of happiness to a single instant, hoping to make it eternal. (What a loss of moments.)

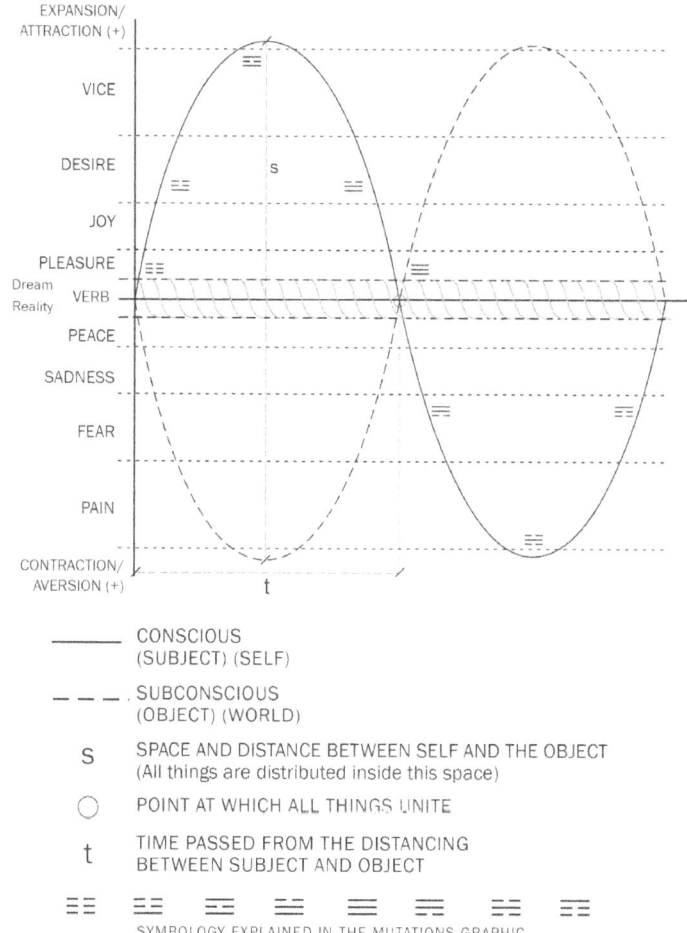

One curve is fantasy. The other, reality. One is the subject who observes. The other, the object observed. Myself, and the world. The distance between these two curves is the very field of our lives—the space between World, God, and Self.

Thought directs the force that molds the world. When we are ruled by the force of feeling—whether pleasant or painful—and act from it, we've relegated thought to the margins. It then appears outside us, seeking to restore balance through someone or something else, demanding clarity, decisions, understanding. Conversely, when thought dominates, it is feeling that returns to demand its share—yearning for freedom, fluidity, love. Reason and Passion make use of matter, which we all are, in order to relate to one another.

Even a simple argument reveals this inner conflict. If I insist, "This is how it is, yes, yes, yes," and the other replies, "No, it isn't, no, no, no," and we each keep pressing our view, it's clear neither of us sees the whole. If reality truly aligned with my claim, it would act accordingly—without conflict or need for persuasion. But even when I convince the other, something unsettled remains—an echo of the negation that was dismissed. That negation may return, later, through an unexpected event that cancels out the former truth. What we call true today may not be tomorrow. And so we continue until opposites are reconciled, until we accept the relativity of our affirmations.

Every conscious affirmation is accompanied, not before nor after, but at the same time, by an unconscious negation. It may be unconscious to us but conscious to the one we confront. Neither can come first, for they interpenetrate each other. We live through the good, then the bad, then the good again, and so on… but day and night arise at the same time the moment a planet is set to drift—or any body set into motion. If we identify with only part of the body, we will suffer day or night. If we identify with the entire planetary body, we remain untouched. And if we identify with the sun and the space beyond, everything changes—we become the walker and the path.

What I highlight, what I speak of, what draws my attention, springs from the Word, which both unites and divides.

According to this Word, we receive responses from aspects beyond our control. This is why it is wise to counter our harsh opinions with kinder ones—to glimpse the beginning, middle, and end of each verb, and know that its good and bad revolve between us both. If the mouth speaks the good or evil of others, over time, we become what we describe. And if we speak of our own good or evil, we pass it on, and another will arise—better or worse.

It's natural to speak of goodness, virtue, and love. But it's ignorance—perhaps even harmful—to press them too forcefully, to shout them until we drag the listener's ears through the dust, and then feel sorry for not being heard. If we say that life is about having a partner, children, planting a tree, writing a book—and that everyone must settle down, and better still if their partner is blonde, rich, and famous—or if we say life is about following a book or tradition, in both cases, we are over-affirming love, giving it form, defining and shaping it according to fantasy or memory. Perhaps we recall a feeling so vividly it revives just by remembering it. But if we are bound to its images and emotional tremors, we are distorting love to our whims—when it is present everywhere and belongs to every form.

What we desire only feels good in the moment we desire it. Once obtained, it leaves behind a hollow—perhaps to be filled by a new quest.

If we walk in nature and find a scene that strikes us like a painting—captivating, beautiful—we may wish to be part of it, even possess it. But upon arriving, we find nothing special. In truth, it looked or felt more magnificent from afar. The same is true of people and things—we first fall in love with a shoulder, a crease, a contrast, a glint, a phrase, a movement... and then—anything becomes possible.

Thought begins from its highest happiness. The self is split between what it encounters and that joy. Then it weaves, in its intricate net of possibilities, an experience that could express that joy, or lead it there once more—through a situation, another person, or an object. We imagine, with all the free will we are capable of, that we can obtain happiness. Fascinating! Thus we affirm a great many things by enjoying their nearness. We look at what we place in front of us, we like it, it pleases us—we enjoy affirming.

Then we have a choice: either we accelerate the movement and become joyful in the presence of what we face, or we remain in delight, carried passively by it. Rather than rising into joy, we descend within. This descent is the quiet acceptance that all is fleeting and transitory. In considering that, we return to union—to happiness—then to peace. Peace is the feeling opposite to delight, yet of equal intensity. While delight affirms, peace is a momentary withdrawal—a gentle negation, a rest from all things. Delight is active—it reaches. Peace is passive—it retreats. These are the first feelings that follow a moment of fullness.

When reality and fantasy approach God, they blend in such a way that rigid matter softens, and something light and free—imagination—is allowed expression. This is the dream world. But the dream world has its own rules, and not all is lovely there. Though these are consciousnesses closer to God, they are not yet united with God. Some delight in creating horrors simply because they now know they aren't real—they enjoy them like a film.

We might dwell in that dream world, but we return to waking life for love of these earliest feelings—pleasure, and peaceful satisfaction. First, one delights in the affirmation of love. Then, it is enough. One withdraws and rests in peace, which momentarily abstains from love—or what we symbolize as such—in order to be satisfied and return to self. And so, we eventually return to affirmation.

In this way, we generate a curve that spans only from delight to peace. The distance we place between ourselves and what we confront is minimal. When I delight, the other is at peace. When I am at peace, the other delights. The wisdom of elders lies in having found this tranquility.

To each feeling corresponds its opposite, which manifests through the world of ideas or things that confront us. These can exchange at any moment through mutual communication.

But if we take the other path, it is because this felt joy no longer suffices. Sweetly stirred, we grow cheerful—our delight begins to shine outward, our affirmation flares, and our one-sided thought swells with euphoria and exuberance. The one who embodies joy confronts sorrow. Where someone is more of something, another will always be less. They generate each other.

Within joy itself, sorrow is seeded. All rage is gathered through excitement. All shame is exposed by excessive curiosity. We rarely notice this in daily life.

This exuberant affirmation can be sated. It can glimpse the other side, draw near, embrace it in fullness—then find peaceful satisfaction.

Yet often, after such joy, the retreat into peace deepens. The Word—or action taken—or let us say love—no longer responds. It has withdrawn. We miss it. We grieve. We've lost the image in which we once recognized it. Lacking reason, we begin to negate with greater force. We conclude: There is no more love. What we once felt—we cannot feel again. We deny what we once affirmed—and all this, we think, against our will. When sorrow has finally exhausted us, negation begins to fade. It no longer matters. "It cannot be," we say, "that this situation still holds me in such despair."

And so, gently, we find calm—once more immersed in peace. And peace, by its silent grace, satisfies us in the simple act of accepting what is…, until once again, we return to delight, dreaming of things we love, and thus the wheel of wonder begins to turn anew.

But negation can deepen still further. "Love will never return. I'm going to lose this or that which brings it. It can't be. I must do something." Fear begins. Something seems to oppose love. Something wants to take it from me—from all of us. I may blame someone, a situation, or some part of myself. "Something threatens me… something strange, something I feel is not me—and I want to push it away, cast it off, get rid of it as quickly as I can."

Then comes despair—born from the unchecked ambition of vanity. It is the night of self-exaltation, of greed. If this negation continues, it turns into pain. Only when we are full of pain do we raise our eyes again—to something higher—confessing our powerlessness. And so we begin again.

Just as we move from delight to peace, so too from fear to desire. One affirms and leaps toward what it wants. The other negates and flees what threatens it. Both hold the same intensity—this is why they are so often intertwined. Desire lurks beneath fear of losing something. Fear flees, driven by the desire to retain it. Thus they complete one another, orbiting the verb we've chosen.

If I feel fear, some earlier desire must have stirred it. But now, it's mirrored by an object before me, one that demands something from me—my healing, my wellbeing, my response, my energy, my love, my life. All depends on the intensity of desire.

If desire grows, it leads to obsession, to abuse, addiction, danger. And eventually, fear too will grow within this person, birthing despair, pain, and illness.

If I generate feelings that are too positive toward someone, it may be because I'm underestimating myself—projecting a kind of inner lack onto them. This negative self-regard turns into an idealized vision of the other. At times, they may be able to absorb it, to carry the weight of our unspoken discomfort. But often, the weight is too much, our expectations too affirming, too heavy. And so they retreat. Or disillusion us. Or vanish entirely.

Whenever we say "no," the unconscious replies with a "yes." And when we say "yes," the unconscious replies with "no." Thus, an inverted curve emerges—a true distance between consciousness and unconsciousness, between the self and the world. At first, this growing separation feels pleasant. But when it stretches too far, and the world we long for seems too distant, despair sets in. The curve, having reached the height of affirmation, begins its descent. In the heart of someone once filled with enthusiasm, weariness and tedium begin to creep in.

It may also happen that while feeling well, we suddenly think about what isn't right—something we must or wish to change. Or we dwell on what we love and still don't feel quite right. It's life rebalancing itself. The affirmation that once filled us begins to leave our center, transferring itself outward—into the world. And in exchange, the negation that once lingered outside begins to fill us. The curve descends until contraction dominates. The world grows larger.

Yet no matter how deep the contraction, a time comes when attraction rises again, or what once bothered us no longer does. The curve, still within negation, begins to climb. It ascends toward that balanced joy of dawn—toward the third person. Here, principles that had converged now reverse and part again. When we behold the opposite and accept it just as it is, we achieve balance—and begin anew.

This is day and night. This is nature. We cannot go against it because this rhythm is what we truly chose to be. In happiness, we do not care. We may not even know that we know. And once we understand how it works, all that remains is to loosen our stubbornness, to understand: to reject what I fear or to affirm what I love as absolutes is as false—or as real—as I want it to be. The truth and what truly matters are pristine and essential by their own nature. They need no defense, no pursuit. They are everywhere.

These endless cycles of mental affirmation and negation slowly carve out what we think we are and what we believe we are not. In contemplating the verb to BE, we realize: we are everything that exists, and we are nothing of it—if we revolve freely and wholly around it. But when we divide ourselves, we say: "This body is me. That body over there is another. It isn't me—it belongs to the world. What nonsense is this saying?"

This—one of our most entrenched illusions—is not real, but it is useful for the motion we now inhabit. If we examine the subject-object divide, we see: I am the subject who observes. What I observe is the object. The object is that which I distinguish from myself. I am always the subject. I can never be the object. Even when I say I AM my body, I am merely observing it—feeling it, thinking it, objectifying it. I remain the subject. Not the object of the senses, or of thought, or of feeling. I see from within a body, then conclude that I AM the eye. But I forget: every word, every idea or feeling that I place after "I" is an object that I distinguish from myself. I may affirm it or negate it, but it is not me. It is not the subject. Which is why: if I am sad or joyful—I am not truly myself. If the body sings or suffers, it is not MY song, nor MY pain, however attached I may feel. I can become this body that sings and suffers—and indeed we all do so to experience life. But in essence, by definition—I am none of this. I cannot see the one who sees.

Who, then, am I?

I am the who.

And in granting full identity to every being—through the name by which I call them, and the action by which I relate to them—I draw the distance that now stands between us, shaped by what I have kept for myself... and so I await their echo, their effect, their reply.

If only we understood: when I am joyful, someone else is sad. And I need not feel guilty for this. Because if I were sad, another would be joyful at the expense of my sorrow. This dead-end leads to a profound silence—the resting place of wisdom. And when balance is lost, wisdom looks upon us with compassion and seeks to keep the distance no greater than that between joy and peace—for our sake.

We can know how it feels to be what confronts us when we understand how we ourselves feel—it is the same, but turned in the opposite direction. If I want nothing from the object, then the feeling I experience seems to come from it. It wants me. But if I want something from the object, the feeling arises within me—robbing the object of feeling, which will likely mirror the opposite and want nothing from me.

Only through communication can we feel the same. The current turns, flows. The distance closes. We no longer know who felt what first. We are delightfully confused. We see ourselves in the other—experiencing both sides, reflecting each other. When we dwell in plenitude, where all becomes one, we fuse. I vanish. So does the other. Only plenitude remains.

When one makes another feel bad—regardless of reason—it is only because they are desperate to feel good. So they transfer their discomfort and keep the pleasure for themselves. The satisfaction a thief feels from stealing equals the pain felt by the victim—and the thief will carry that pain in time.

And one who makes another feel good is often postponing themselves. By showing themselves in inferior condition, they elevate the other. Everyone feels good around them—except the giver, who suffers from long self-denial, until the day of harvest arrives.

These tendencies give rise to two primary currents of personality: some place themselves after others, some before; some tend toward pessimism, others toward optimism; some are drawn to action, others to stillness; some proclaim duty, others desire—some guard the boundary, others chase freedom.

The one who proclaims duty is, in truth, always placing himself first—offering advice, acting according to his own will and belief in what is best, wherever he pleases, even in places where it is not his place to act. And the one who proclaims freedom is always placing himself last—tending to step aside, to let others be, encouraging them, assisting them in exercising their liberty. Though this is not always what's needed—for in the name of my freedom, I might run headlong into a heavy fall, had no one cared to warn me.

This battle of personalities is the reflection of the deeper struggle—between thought and feeling, between the self and the world.

And so, those who voluntarily took on suffering and responsibility for the sake of their people were named saints. They conjured evil with a nameless simplicity—halting its spread, silencing its effect.

A life is not fulfilled until it contemplates the opposite within. One who is fulfilled is one who accepts the present, accepts themselves and others as they are—and stops believing that their neighbor is a threat or that their own ideology is salvation.

Each of our daily encounters is a dance of affirmations and negations—emotional and mental. I may be face-to-face with someone who feels as bad as I do—but they're on the same side of negation. We are not facing each other. We are facing something else—something good. There is no escape. Only when one stops clinging to either affirmation or negation does fullness emerge. Then the path appears.

If I insist that reality must be as I believe it to be, I do not consider the response I will receive. Just as if I declared all words meaningless—we would cease to speak. We'd grunt like animals. Perhaps even descend into despair. In both cases, I see only one side. Yet both exist. Every reader, every listener, brings their own meaning. Their own reality, unlike our own.

Reconciliation lies only in accepting the opposite—within the joy of the Word, which creates and holds both sides. Which is why: nothing we do is truly done by us. It is the Word acting in us, for us. And yet—if we were the ones doing, we'd learn something. We'd know the science of action and reaction, of work and reward, of good and evil.

So if we wish for plenitude to keep doing all things, the shortest path is flow with acceptance, and let go. This is why: "What is, is not—and so it is said to be."

In acceptance, one can affirm or negate—even desire—without problem. Because there is no urge to change. Change comes by itself. There is no thirst for gain, for he knows he is already whole. No difference divides him, no loss touches his fullness. He is with God—or simply, he is.

When we slip beyond the enchantment of an experience that takes hold of the imagination — a flicker of the unknown, a ripple not yet named — our thoughts and feelings fall into place, anchored in the now. All conclusions fade like footprints in water. There is no affirmation, no denial, no knowing of the known, no knower. In that moment, joy arrives unannounced, not by what surrounds us, but through the absence of the one who surrounds it. The self forgets itself — not by erasing, but by softening its edges until even its questions grow quiet. Nothing vanishes. Rather, everything agrees to be. Thought and feeling, past and future, yes and no, meet at the same threshold, fold into each other, and become one seamless field of presence — undivided, untouched, whole.

Without doubt, after that spark of happiness we begin to affirm. But the affirmation comes after the spark—after that instant of enchantment in which we were whole. Such experiences can arise anywhere, at any time. Though they come unbidden, we seek to repeat them, returning to the places where we once felt them, or to the rituals others promise will lead us there again: meditation, prayer, singing, art, sex, concerts, stadiums, drugs, alcohol, recovery, fashion, travel, alarms, monasticism, even suicide. Or perhaps simply the absence of action. We all long to relive the moment, and we imagine how it would be.

When one forgets oneself, the boundary between the self and the world vanishes. One becomes the landscape, the sound, the child, the phrase, the other, the idea, the feeling, the life, the death, the universe, God—or whatever name we give to the unity. But when we wish that what stands before us be different than it is—better, worse, anything but this—then love is absent. What remains is attachment, affection, interest, but not love. We love more our image of how things should be than what is. In that instant, we sever the thread of union and step into the role of modification, resisting the sacrifice that all change requires.

When I remember myself as a personality, it rises between me and the world, between me and happiness. If I remember myself with pride, then God help us, for I have become dangerous. And so, detachment, surrender, the forgetting of demands, of self-image, of division—these are the sacred acts taught by every religion. They bring us closer to agreement and unity, letting happiness build for us a home. Even the scientist must forget himself, so that his gaze does not cloud the purity of the experiment with the dust of his presence—for only in silence does truth reveal its unbroken form.

Some will argue we must chase our dreams and assert our will. But the truth is, when we are full and truly happy, dreams and desires fall away. In this dual world, the daily sacrifice of being grants us the right to dream, to long to understand what all this means. But even dreams and desires, at their core, seek happiness. And though happiness is everywhere, it feels like the hardest thing to find. Others even will claim that pure innocence leaves us vulnerable, easy to manipulate. But such fears belong to those who won't leap, trembling on the high dive, too afraid to fall. True innocence carries its own quiet strength, an uncanny instinct for survival—and it drifts, almost by nature, toward lighter realms: more subtle, less dense, like the hush before waking from a dream.

As we see life everywhere, we must also see death—and that which holds them both. Then, transcending all three, we arrive at the One in whom neither life nor death are truly real, for all is an eternal, changing now.

In the moment of joy, we do not think, "How happy I am." We simply are. But soon we begin to crave that moment again, and in doing so, we become dependent on the experiences that gave rise to it. Thus duality begins: we affirm one experience and reject another. We become hunters of experiences.

Desire, in its pursuit of happiness, is rooted in fear of our present state—thus, the problem lies not in the experience itself, but in the duality born from our conclusions. Duality exists, yes, but it is not the truth. The truth is what holds the duality. Experience is always whole, always full, regardless of whether it delights or displeases us. When one knows this, one stops clinging to "yes" and "no," knowing they only lead us away from love, truth, and self. We stop insisting, "I this..." and "They that..." We act, but lightly, without attachment.

For those who do not know this, effort is needed—to sort, to divide, to organize one's values. Our only real work is to carry the invisible pack where we store our favorite affirmations and denials—those we want to guide our lives, those we fight for. We separate what belongs to one side, and what to the other: symbols, sensations, events. The problem arises when the two sides face each other—the demander and the demanded, the self and the world, the wave and the particle—and do not recognize themselves as complementary, as arbitrary reflections of a greater whole.

Then we mistake happiness for something that belongs to a memory, to an experience we wish to repeat. These conclusions write a script for the self, a program of habits, a protocol for when happiness is allowed to arrive.

The self is always seeking a safe space to be different without risk. In the predictable rhythm of habit, nothing unexpected can occur. But the universe unfolds in endless possibility. Still, we see only what we choose to see. We cling to habit as a point of reference, lest we lose ourselves in the undefined. The primary habit is life itself: to wake, to bathe, to eat, to work, to wander, to rest. But we have many more. We identify with them, cling to them, for without habit there is no memory, and without memory we do not recognize ourselves.

And so, there is no true obligation to respond to those we encounter with any particular reaction—positive, negative, or neutral. Only the habit obliges us. We feel pain or pleasure not because the person or situation warrants it, but because our memory has made it so. Yet we hold within us the power to reverse these habits. We can feel pain where once there was pleasure, and pleasure where once there was pain. Not that we must—it is neither necessary nor advised. Should we love labor and hate festivals? Shall we play the madman, the fakir?

The nervous self clings to absolutes. To it, success, wealth, fame, power, victory—these must always delight, just as sugar must always be sweet. Rejection, failure, loneliness, impotence, accidents—these must always bring sorrow. But one need not grieve at every loss. One can meet misfortune with stillness. A touch may be welcome or unbearable—not only to different people, but even to the same person, in different times. Lovers today may be litigants tomorrow. A needle may evoke fear—until we learn it carries the cure. The nervous self is enslaved to habit. To vary its responses is to veer into the unknown, into what seems abnormal. And so it clings to its scripts, shaping its personality by repetition.

Thus, thought is bound only to the extent that it chooses to be. It dwells in one mental habit rather than another. Only through self-observation can those habits begin to change.

> *When one tries to catch a thought, it slips away. If we fall into silence, thought falls silent too. We wait for one to arise—but as long as our gaze remains fixed and unyielding, none will come. We are left in stillness. And without knowing how, we soon find ourselves in the midst of yet another thought—unable to pinpoint the moment we gave in, nor the reason it emerged. The same happens with feelings. With things. Even scientists, when they face matter head-on, find no solid thing, only a condensation of energy, they say. And when I turn my attention to the energy I feel, seeking some pure or divine sensation—I find nothing. Or rather: I find myself, in all three cases with the unknown. And the unknown is me—not what I think, nor*

what I feel, nor what I see. I am not the known. I am the knower. And the knower cannot be known. If I knew who I was, I wouldn't truly be myself.

I am the eternally unknowable.

When I desire an object, it is because I know it only in part—what draws me is the fragment still cloaked in mystery.

And once I come to know the part I did not know, the charm begins to fade. What calls to me is the mystery—and the mystery of mysteries is none other than myself, reflected, projected, suspended in the form of an object.

This reflex is born with the individual, and flows from his unity—which is the Word, which is God. And only later does the personality claim it for its own delight.

Each moment rises as a singular spark, original and unrepeatable, no matter how stubbornly I or any artist might try to recreate it. What does not change is me—eternal, unmoving—inseparably bound to the ever-changing, all-powerful God. How it must be, and how I secretly wish it to be, is already happening. Even if the flavor of life is not knowing it.

globalized wisdom of the XXI century

- treatise II -

The elements, and their mutations

All conflict arises when one resists feeling what is felt, thinking what is thought, or living what unfolds. When we long to think in one way and not another, to feel "That" and not this, we oppose the real with the ideal. Thus emerges a double "I": the one who longs for "That," and the one who bears "This." The problem lies in our identification—with images, thoughts, or emotions.

At the beginning, we hold the right to all things—but we lose it the moment we cling to any particular one. This identification narrows our gaze, fixating our being within a single perspective of life. To recover the full truth of ourselves, we must journey through the continual exchange between two visions of existence: from subject to object and object to subject, from reality to fantasy and back, from the absolute to the relative and again to the absolute, from life to death and death to life, from space to time and time to space, from me to you and you to me. This movement—which is the Verb, the Third Person, the current flowing between first and second, between you and me, object and subject—is the intrinsic relationship of all things. This is why the Trinity is called Holy.

When I no longer recognize the object as part of myself, and instead see it as wholly separate, I generate the division that casts shadows—the beginning of a point of view. The being leans into an apparent separation through which relationships are defined and held apart, face to face, that they might meet again and reunite. Thus arises the delight of separation and of contact, played out within a unity of rhythm and pause. We behave as persons among persons, yet remain always in the indivisible unity of being. For both you and I are held within the single, unshakable truth of existence.

Unity—or happiness—unfolds through the Verb, whose vibration generates subjects and objects: the knower and the known within knowledge, the lover and the beloved within love. The other is none but myself, inverted—a shadow of the light that gives rise to both. For seeing to occur, there must be an object, a subject, and the instrument—the eye and the act of seeing. Just as cause, instrument, and effect are one, so too are the lover, the love, and the beloved; the mind, the plenitude, and the body are inseparable.

When the Verb aligns solely with the subject, it becomes centered in "me," the conscious self—and I am the one who acts, who knows, who loves, who moves. But when the Verb empowers the object, then knowledge manifests through events and outcomes; the other becomes the actor, the one who knows, the one who loves—and I may feel out of place or confused. The object becomes the reference point, the bearer of meaning, the apparent source of the Verb.

Yet when the Verb is free, belonging neither to subject nor object, it flows as pure energy in the plenitude of their union—harmony between life and mind. A practical metaphor: two people dancing in unison, moving together in something greater than themselves. When love belongs to no one, it spins freely between them, drawing them close. But to love one thing too much is to trap love inside oneself, to mold it inwardly, stifling its flow. It grows into a fantasy, detached from reality, and this inner tension eventually reflects outward as denial or loss. Letting go, embracing cool objectivity or humbly

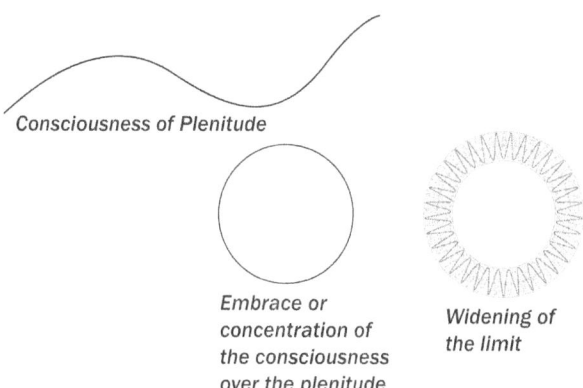

Consciousness of Plenitude

Embrace or concentration of the consciousness over the plenitude

Widening of the limit

The amplitude of the plenitude and the conscience that crosses it can be represented by a simple line in space. The space is attracted to the line and the line to space, so the line embraces the space. In this way, a line generates two spaces, and these look to join together in a line, generating the broadening of the previous one in a third space common to the first two, which produces vibration and another two apparent limit lines.

In this way, an apparent inside and outside are generated, which are the same only plenitude looked through that widened and spatialized conscience. It's the volume, the body, the eye that looks at that same line of conscience that orbits the plenitude but needing to travel across it to reach it.

Then we have four movements, three spaces and two outlines that are the volume of the Trinity, the force of Duality, the conscience of Unity

admitting our powerlessness, allows love to emerge again—this time from outside, as grace.

God is love, and love is everywhere. One cannot seek what is already all around. Nor can one escape it or deny it, for wherever there is a place or a time, there too is God. Life is the path of loving God—first in others, and later, beyond the forms of others, in the Eternal Unity we all share. If mere folds of form can so enthrall us that we lose our minds and selves to them, how will we ever stand with strength before God Himself, maker of all folds and all forms?

Knowledge, split into knower and known, moves between them, creating vibration and time. You, I, and the Verb that travels back and forth: we are the wheel of time. I speak, then the world responds. I rule, then the world rules me. I know, then another knows. Though knowledge exists on its own, it seems to alternate through us. From this, it follows that in the stillness of my purest self, I long for, seek, and emulate that which surpasses me—God, or whatever bears His likeness. And on the other side of the veil, God longs for me as well, seeks me, and each day brings me back, as if returning me to my origin. This mutual reaching creates a living relief, a flowing reflection that slowly shapes the contours of existence—sculpting life from the silent play of shadow and light. Yet unless we learn to see, we go on separating ourselves from That, imagining it as a stranger who loves us, hates us, or remains indifferent. When in truth... we are all That—the One, reflecting itself through every face, in every illusion of division.

Thus, two paths emerge in how we relate to the world:

If the Verb dwells in the Object, then I lean toward what is known—the world of tangible things. I become enchanted by ideal forms, by figures and situations that seem perfect to me. I fall in love with what I behold—the second person—and devote myself to pursuing that which I admire, the outer image of my longing.

But if the Verb resides in the Subject, then I become its bearer. I am the one who carries its fire, and by that flame, I shape the world to my own image. I become the reason, the purpose, the benefit of others. I am the force and the will, the pulse of movement and meaning that binds me to you—the third person, alive between us.

At times, I take myself for the body—and thus begin the long pilgrimage toward the spirit. At others, I believe I am the spirit—and strive to bend the body and the world to my will. But in the stillness before belief, before name and thought arise, I am the One behind all things—the silent Witness, the breathless axis around which every force and form turns. I am the clear and boundless light, before it ever reflects itself into being.

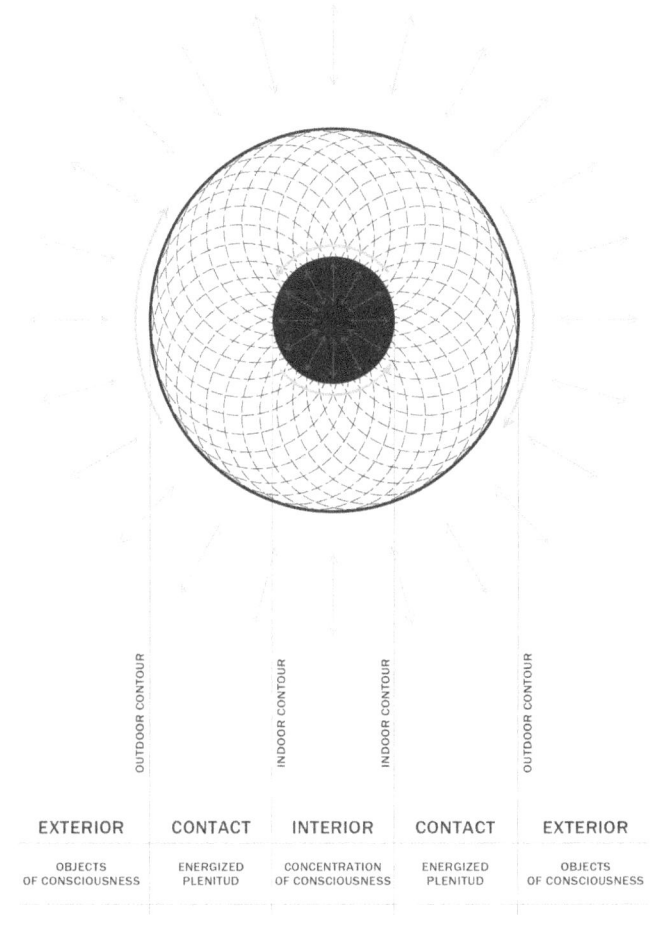

EXTERIOR	CONTACT	INTERIOR	CONTACT	EXTERIOR
OBJECTS OF CONSCIOUSNESS	ENERGIZED PLENITUD	CONCENTRATION OF CONSCIOUSNESS	ENERGIZED PLENITUD	OBJECTS OF CONSCIOUSNESS

We all pass through these movements and mindsets, whether we will it or not; it is the nature of human being. Thus when events leave us stunned, mind blank, breath still—or when someone asks something we do not know and we fall into ignorance—then the sleeping darkness stirs. The silence of unchanging consciousness emerges, and we stand before the Unknown. God eclipses us in cold and darkness, disguised as meaninglessness. We are left without power, without love, without being: in nothingness. This happens when the Verb has passed entirely into the object confronting us—to which we once gave power, by loving or hating it, by projecting thought and will upon it.

It is but a balancing mechanism—so that both subject and object might return to the place that is no place, and in longing for that place, find again the revelation of being whole. A new day. A new knowledge that unites. A truth that transcends. New senses, new essences, a new distance between self and world. And so, out of the object, the Verb returns to us—bringing relief. In matter we behold light. In events, a birth. In others, the one who carries truth, or help, or solution. Only when we empty ourselves completely can we behold the whole.

This movement of possibility expresses itself now as force of emotion, now as awareness of thought, now as physical sensation—providing multiple perspectives through which we may play the game of human existence.

The halting and focusing of being on a single point within the whole gives rise to the division: I-see-that. The world and I become the two faces of the same sacred Verb: to see, to be, to live, to know, to love—whichever it may be. Each of us then takes from what stands before us and reflects it inwardly, forming our own minor trinity, our own private world: three persons in the singular, mirrored in three more in the plural. I borrow a form and an action and adopt them as my own. I imitate that spontaneous moment of union between body, mind, and life—that fleeting glimpse of happiness. Feeling secure, I try to possess it, to repeat it at will. Each individual shapes their uniqueness from these brief illuminations, flashes of bliss caught in the net of the mind; and so, many come to believe that it was this object or that action which caused their joy. These impressions linger in memory, and through them we relate to others, comparing and distinguishing, generating a subtle distance—a meaning and a sensation that we assign to the objects, a "how it looks" and a "how it feels" in the synthesis of our judgments.

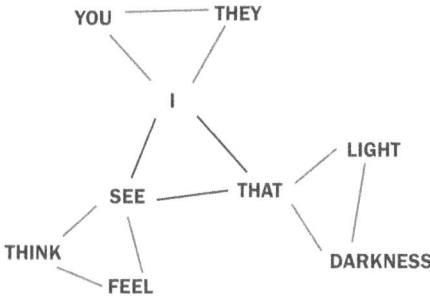

Knowledge, at first, simply is or is not. Therefore, it belongs to no one when the Trinity is present; or to both, when Unity appears. As knowledge moves between subject and object, it generates the flow of before and after. The Verb becomes temporal, seemingly mine, or seemingly the object's. If I know nothing, I will find light; but if I believe I know everything, I will meet only darkness. When the motion of knowing reaches a twilight midpoint between subject and object, we glimpse the unity within the Trinity. When it moves toward or away, we are drawn to it, or it to us.

This generates a second unfolding of unity, revealing four concurrent stances, alternating between the outer realm (matter) and the inner realm (spirit or point of view). Some postures manifest, others observe, suspended in time—for while the first division arises in space, the second arises in time. If we use the verb "to know" as an example, the four elemental positions are:

I know, and That knows — Air, Day
I know, and That does not know — Fire, Dawn
I do not know, and That knows — Water, Dusk
I do not know, and That does not know — Earth, Night

First come the dominions of the elements. Later, living beings and human figures arise, creating further divisions within each. We understand that, in essence, the "I" is not any

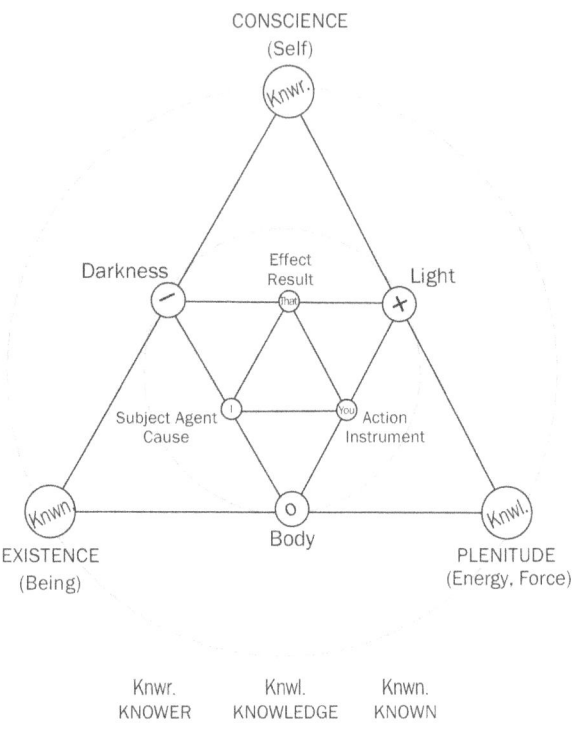

Knwr.   Knwl.   Knwn.
KNOWER   KNOWLEDGE   KNOWN

particular form of life; the self may adopt whatever form it chooses, but never for long. Miraculously, when we cease to know, we begin to learn. And conversely, when I seize upon a single action, I interrupt the freedom of the object's movement. It halts, becomes available to receive, to be transformed. So too, people on the other side of the world: when they sleep, they leave the work to us. When we sleep, they awaken. Every object upon which we act will, in time, awaken in its own movement and return to us the echo of what we once did to it.

Just as the one who listens is not the one who speaks, so too the beloved cannot love us while we insist on being the lover. If I am consumed with desire for someone, they may bask in the flattery of their ego, but they will never truly love me. To be loved, we must choose, in the presence of love, to attend instead to the necessity of the moment, to shift the focus toward ourselves with humility. Then, the other might observe us—and if we were quietly good, secretly generous—they may be moved to become the lover, drawn toward us as the beloved.

The ideal between lover and beloved is a movement in unison— a current of alternating charge, where opposites draw near and, through the swift rhythm of exchange, dissolve their boundary in the pure motion that guides them. There, at last, they are seen not as two, but as mirrored faces of the same being.

Thus, no matter what we choose, we can never remain solely the lover or the beloved. We cannot always be the speaker, the singer; the world, too, wishes to speak, to sing to us. This reveals itself in everything we do: something unexpected always arises—something beyond our control, something different from what we intended. Even as we sing, we find within the song a voice we did not know was ours: strange, imperfect, but undeniably true. If there are errors, it is because we tried too hard to control the outcome, clinging to a particular good. In response, matter—or perhaps God—gently mocks our selfishness, scattering flaws like mirrors.

So the Verb spinning in our mind is vital. For if I sing, the world will answer with its own secret melody. If I seek to rule, some force will rise to rule me in turn. If I claim to know, a greater knowing will emerge to unmake my certainty. And so the Word, eternal and ungraspable, plays itself through us—as question, as echo, as unfolding law.

Thus, the fourfold current must be held in view—only then does the river of being flow freely and carry us nearer to the opposite. But if one clings to just a single posture, the balance falters, the current slows, and the division deepens—until, at last, the other faces rise in response.

If love binds us to another, we will inevitably pass through all four tides of its motion:

1. We both love.
2. I love, and you do not.
3. You love, and I do not.
4. Neither of us loves.

Every action we undertake turns like this, in cycles of approach and withdrawal. If we can withstand the full arc of that turning, the bond holds—tempered not by certainty, but by our willingness to pass through the shifting truths of love.

Our problems, then, arise from the effect upon which we stand. A cause becomes "cause" only when we accept something as fixed, resolved, and center our awareness upon it as the origin—from which we seek either escape or fulfillment. But in doing so, we fail to see the true cause within us. We simply burn with the urgency to change or resolve a situation, unaware that the result of our results becomes the true cause, and the cause of our causes is born from the result. If I was the cause of another's suffering, then the fruit of that suffering must return to me. And what I have chosen and done with the world—the world will, in turn, do with me. Not out of malice, but simply by mirroring me, by imitating what I myself have shown it to be.

The Verb is a single unfolding in plenitude; and all the I's are one same I, a single space holding all things; and all Those things are one same object, the totality of physical being, the manifest universe. The three—subject, verb, and object—are capable of infinite multiplicity through the mysterious unity of the Holy Trinity; and yet, none can be the other. Each holds its place so that existence may be. I am not you, nor he or she, nor the action nor its result, neither sky nor earth, neither love nor the loved—yet the three persons are always present, everywhere, at once.

When Unity is: feeling and thought dissolve their forms. For when the being is whole and in bliss, it distinguishes no objects within the whole—it is one with all. And in a subtler unfolding of this always-same reality, we notice that thoughts persist, even as the physical world melts away. And our first thought, upon awakening there, is: "I am all."

When division arises: unity condenses itself to uphold thought in its tension with feeling. It mentalizes to sustain feeling as it confronts the world. It energizes to uphold thought as it confronts the world. Feelings form thoughts, thoughts form feelings, and forms feel and think. In times of conflict, thought slips—from dividing to being divided—and becomes tangled in its own webs and workings. The being forgets the simple truth: that all thoughts are one consciousness taking differing views; all feelings, the same plenitude in varied currents of intensity; my body and all surrounding bodies— one same nature of action, dancing the endless interplay of force and awareness, of feeling and thinking, of you and me.

The pure idea is born in unity; it unfolds, and resolves into a particular feeling with a given force. That feeling becomes a movement and resolves into what I see—shaping matter or creating life's situations. Thus the seen is born, becomes effect, and resolves into the one who sees: into me. I shape my thoughts by affirming or denying this result, identifying only with certain parts of what appears. A synthesis of memory and imagination over reality, that resolves again in a particular feeling. This felt force generates a movement that adjusts more closely to the prior thought, shaping images that resemble the original idea. Then thought begins to repeat, revolving and refining that action, energizing and perfecting it again and again. Matter emerges from energy, energy from consciousness, and consciousness from its union with them. All new life and movement will arise within the scope of our consciousness, and within the ideas in which we place the faith and force of our present motion.

Even the slightest thought precipitates matter. If, for example, I think of someone, "What a fool," and linger in that conclusion—it generates a certain feeling, one that matter absorbs and spins until it manifests a future moment in which I see myself as the fool, and someone walks by mirroring my former attitude. If we can glimpse our own clumsiness in the clumsiness of others, we may guide them gently, and thus balance the force. But trouble arises if we believe ourselves immune. It's not that fools don't exist—but their foolishness is shared. It is the awareness of a temporary state, which, if we give it just a bit more attention, transforms.

The energy born of feeling becomes the ground where matter takes shape, and from that reshaped matter, a new path of meaning unfolds back to thought.

When I feel a great urge to change something, it means energy has thinned on the other side. The excited self draws more force for itself, leaving less for others. The wiser path is to act like a good father or teacher: having the upper hand, yet approaching and guiding to restore balance, so all may live in peace. What's most sensible is to work for the other to function. In doing so, our excess energy flows outward and the scales are evened.

When we become overcharged with desire and cling too tightly to a single form, imagination and longing begin to multiply—perhaps we expect a person to behave according to our ideals, or we impose on our children the dreams we never fulfilled, or we simply crave to possess beautiful things. This excitement lifts us with euphoria and boldness on one side, yet binds us in growing dependence on the other. We hunger more and more for what, in the end, will bring suffering—because existence, being wider than any single thing, eventually seeks to shake off limitation. Yet surely, that very thing will come to us, in time and in some form, especially if we offer it up, speak it, give it away—this is the reason for honesty, the mystery of prayer, the grace of confession—for expression gives fluidity to the creative current. When we breathe our energy into something or someone and release it without grasping, it will, in time, find its way back—

depleted, drawn again to the source that once filled it with light. Thus, we must allow the cycle to complete itself, and be ready to begin anew—diving once more into the tortuous, meandering current of thoughts and feelings, and into the contortions born from the struggle of the "I" that lost its true nature in an object, only to recover itself through the very act of losing. So that every error may be refined into truth—since both truth and error are but the curved edges of our own distortion; so that every sorrow in plenitude—like our pain and our joy—may fulfill its trembling labor of sensation; so that every impotence in power—like our weakness and our strength—may reveal itself as the force striving to be; and every death in immortality—toward which life and death are both but ceaseless efforts of experience.

The first thing we come to know about you and me is that we relate to one another through a movement shaped by threefold expression: feeling, thinking, and the physical senses. In this, we recognize a trinity within our being—sentiments, sensations, and thoughts—through which we move in our ongoing process of renewal and transformation. We also come to see that in states of happiness or unity, there can be no difference between your feeling and mine, your thought and mine, your matter and mine. Feeling simply is. Matter simply is. And in the purity of experience, no word can fully capture who we are, for what is revealed is the unity of mind, body, life—or all three as one.

True solitude belongs only to this unity, which is God, for only God is originally one in all. But we, wherever we find ourselves, will always encounter at least three presences: the Self, the Word, and the Object; the first, second, and third persons, each made omnipresent through that indivisible unity. I will always be before you, even if our forms change. You will always be there, looking upon me, wherever I may appear. And there will always be some love about which you and I may speak, some thread we may manifest, and become eternal within it. Reality is first imagined, then believed, and at last—despite all disbelief—known.

We have said that our being, for delight, mutates from union to division, separating only to reunite. So even if I and That seem divided, we are two faces of the same unity—we are not independent. If I claim independence from That, I give reality to That, for without it, independence has no meaning. Freedom requires something to be free from—otherwise, freedom vanishes. And if, on the contrary, I say I am nothing, and only That is real and worthy of worship, I fall again into duality—for even That needs the silent regard of the subject who observes and energizes. By intrinsic unity, That can never be apart from me, though the veils may try to deceive.

We are the subjects of material unfolding. But in immersing ourselves in human life, we become objects. Subjects become objects, and objects again become subjects. They spin around one another until union comes. They change one into the other. They do not vanish. So when something is lost, and That is gone from us, we at last become subjects again—for we had lost ourselves in an object. Thus the mind comes to serve the body. And in becoming subjects again, a transformation occurs in the mind—it cleanses, it empties, it opens itself to a new reality. What was lost in matter passes into mind. Through our will, we were lost in That. Now That is lost—and reborn in us—infusing the spirit with guiding ideas. The unity is never disturbed. True plenitude is never lost. The Verb is merely transformed. Whether I am with, against, or without That—it remains, holding me and That alike.

An object is necessary for the dance between force and awareness. But any object will do—whether a universe or a particle, especially those of a subtler nature than human form. Only when we pass from one to the other, embracing both in a shared accord, a breath, a joint action—only then do we begin to assimilate, to unite, to surpass and transfigure—until we glimpse the unity of space in the void of consciousness, where an infinite veil of particles weaves itself together in perfect unison.

The reason we appear to summon actions into being, to conjure brilliant solutions or radiate great force—and likewise, the reason things seem to arise from the void and stir us, or that we are swept up by unwelcome tides and betrayed by our own longings—lies in the silent drift of the adopted Verb. It flows between realms, weaving through the known and the unknown, crossing from hand to hand, as if existence itself were breathing through us and back into the world. Should we hold it—the Verb, the force, the knowing—it will not remain ours. That which we have dared to shape with our will, whether truth or beauty or power, will inevitably pass into the hands of the other side, into the world of things we cannot command. The objects will inherit it. They will become the ones to carry reason, to cradle love, to hold the breath of life and the authority of action. They will unmake what we have made and remake it into their own likeness. And whether this return comes as the same object, or some stranger cloaked in fate, it will come.

There is only one way through: to offer freely. To relinquish what we do and what we desire, not into absence, but into the wholeness—the undivided all that is God. To act for the sake of union, not possession. For when the power of knowing stands on the other shore, it will remember what was once given without price, and it will return the gift.

If we help without expectation, if we give in gratitude without chasing reward, we help restore to each what is most natural—each other, in the purity of being. More deeply still, we draw closer to that mysterious other side, from which the current flows anew, ever refreshing itself. If each of us holds a fragment of the Whole, we must only be honest with one another, never casting away a single shard, so that the cosmic puzzle may complete itself.

From the indivisible unity of being we can say this: when "I" act, "That" does not—it is acted upon. And when "That" acts, "I" am still—I am the one transformed. Unless, of course, we move together in harmony, modifying one another in mutual action. That is the unity within diversity. Or neither acts, and there is peace—that is the diversity within unity.

When the harmony of happiness appears, it asks softly, like a sphinx in silence: "What name do you give this harmony, with which you now identify so completely?" And joyfully, filled with wonder, I answer: "This thing! That place! That person!" But the moment I name it, the fullness departs, flowing toward what I have named. In seeing plenitude only there, I am separated from the plenitude that was here.

Indeed, there is free will. A turning of the wheel where we momentarily hold the rudder—and in that moment we must be cautious, kind, imaginative, compassionate, truthful, generous, attentive, embracing… so that when night falls, that same measure may be used in return.

For just as delight inquires, so too does rage. What we call pleasure is the exhalation of the Whole, the joy of Being tasting itself. What we name hatred is the trembling of all things when unity is forgotten—what mystics have called the wrath of God. Yet neither bliss nor fury belong to anyone. They are winds that move through the soul of the world. And so we are spared the cursed mirror of vengeance, the shadows cast by false honor, those illusions that lead us away—from truth, into conflict, into the sorrow of war.

From the primordial divide of being—idea and force—one might say: when I seize the idea, when I hold its shape within thought, That is the one who feels, who bears the weight of its hidden current. And when I am the one trembling with the force, That becomes the seer, the one who knows why the wave moves, and where it longs to go. Thus we dance across a mirrored field: one soul drawn to thought, another to feeling—or each seeking distance from what stirs too deeply, hoping that in contrast, the self will emerge clear. One leans into becoming, the other into being. One toward the unknown blossom, the other to the old root. One toward the flame of joy, the other toward the coolness of repose.

When I think of That, That inevitably turns inward—assuming the place of the Subject, the place I once held. For in that moment, I have turned outward, projected myself upon the Object, and in doing so, I cease to be the "I" and become That in which I lose myself.

And when I return attention to myself, something turns toward me. Every time I think of myself, there is also a That, feeling me—it may be someone holding a sentiment toward me, or simply God loving me. Similarly, if I pour out a feeling toward someone, it creates in them the one who thinks and knows themselves; or, in the case of an object, it reinforces its form.

We know this because nothing in the whole may vanish. All is implicated in the same unfolding. It's not that one person thinks and the other feels, but that in each encounter there is consciousness, and there is a current of force. And when I occupy one, That must occupy the other.

Just as the whole planet lives both day and night at once, so too, if I take myself to be a person, it is only because there is always another enacting the opposite. This is the very principle behind matter and anti-matter. In the immediacy of the present, when one walks, one also becomes what is walked, for every step forward sets the path behind. Matter moves always in counterpoint to mind,

and when a second person enters, they tend to carry the polarity we left behind. In the dance, as one leads, the other follows, and then the roles reverse. The masculine meets the feminine, and were it not so, we could not know ourselves as persons at all. But when I behold both, I hold the whole. I am the one who walks and the path that is walked. I am one with the objects, flowing in harmony with the movement that arises.

In their purest states, thought, feeling, and form bear no

contradiction. They are one in the Trinity, one in the diversity of Being. But in division, the force of feeling inclines toward some experiences and avoids others. When energy rises on one side, it must fall on the other. Every feeling resolves itself into one of three paths: expansion-force-attraction, contraction-impotence-aversion, or contemplation-harmony-indifference. Either I am drawn to it, or I recoil. Or I fall into indifference—and if I cannot remain in harmony, then I simply behold what is given. This indifference becomes a threshold; it stirs the still waters of the mind and gives birth to thought.

In the division of thought, the I clings to certain ideas and rejects others, handing them over to That. Ideas, actions, and objects appear as mine, or as belonging to another—or else they arise as questions, unanswered, inviting the world of spontaneous matter to offer its reply. And in the division of nature itself, light and darkness alternate, pulsing in countless rhythms and intensities. From this vibration, all physical form is born.

This leads us to a new unfolding—nested within the first division of knower, knowing, and known. The knower splits again: either it is mine, or it is another who knows. Knowledge, too, divides itself into contraction and expansion. And what is known—matter itself—oscillates between light and shadow.

Thus, whether through thought, feeling, or matter, I relate to That affirmatively, negatively, or neutrally. Neutrality holds the balance, standing nearest to the greater term. It grants us the grace of union through action with the opposite. This harmonic and indifferent point may appear as the self, the deed, or the object. It may be spoken in thoughts, or whispered in feelings, or shown in what we see. The other two gather around this still point, forming their own trinity, growing a body of affirmation, or negation.

The objects we see are reflections of ourselves. This is why, if we think well of someone, eventually someone will appear who thinks well of us. Yet both they and we may feel some discomfort in the space between one moment of well-being and another. The more I love a "special" person, the more the "non-special" ones will charge me for that specialness. And the more someone affects me, the more they will bask in their pride, feeling empowered over many things. We all know life is transitory, yet we continue to build our "special ones" as if they could last forever. All people are the same one self. Thus, the wise path is not to judge That as good or bad, but to become one with the good and the bad of That—this is compassion: placing ourselves in the other and move toward balance and unity.

If we accept the praise and expectations of others as truth—whether about ourselves or someone else—we inherit burdens, responsibilities we did not seek, sacrifices to endure, hardships to pass through, and only after another cycle may we be rewarded. Still less should we accept negative judgments—especially those from people who, in declaring our goodness false, claim goodness solely for themselves. Some believe they are so good that they feel justified in punishing others in the name of their supreme virtue. But in truth, anyone who gratuitously and without cause points out flaws in others is likely on the brink of committing a great error.

It hardly matters which object I choose to focus on. Whether I deem light or darkness "good," I always place the "good" on my side, and I will always encounter more of what I label as good—though some of those things may uplift me, and others drag me down. Thus, I become the consequence, the fruit, of what I see as good. Each to their preferred object. But if that object is not truly theirs, if it is too ambitious—placed by the imagination in a distant and difficult place—the price will be high: sacrifice, struggle, endurance. That hardship is simply the distance I have placed between myself and what I desire.

If I wish to go toward That, I must leave This. If I long for daylight, I must endure the night—and vice versa. The way I choose to approach That is indifferent in itself. It is a single flow, branching into countless currents. Through any of them, the day arrives just the same. Even the object of desire, once let go, returns in time on its own.

Whatever I do produces effects: delight, displeasure, or undifferentiated questioning. But the true value lies where I, the action, and the object become One. The real problem arises when I believe that a particular action or object that once brought union is the sole bearer of unity. That belief draws me deeper into a private world of dependence on specific things or situations. Yet even having lost that unity, the surest way to remember it is through acts of contemplation, understanding, and love. These draw us naturally toward oneness. They are the primary gestures of the senses, of thought, of feeling. We may also meditate on an object that represents God or the transcendent. In doing so, we may come to embody That, even if at first it feels fantastic or impossible. But if we focus on limited things, we shall suffer their limitations when the cycle turns again.

The unity of the year divides into four seasons:
1. I say yes to That.
2. I say no to That.
3. That says yes to me.
4. That says no to me.

Just as the self first identifies with union or separation, it later identifies with one of these four. Taking it as real and absolute, it fashions it into a body and must then move through the remaining three possibilities. Many people live their entire lives within one of these four stances, constantly resisting or justifying themselves before the others—even though we all experience all four. We become truly conscious only when we know this and refrain from clinging to any one stance.

Where division exists, these four points of view can always be found, acting and interacting. The degree to which I insist on any of them will determine the nature of my relationships. When the insistence is obsessive, one leads a violent life. When it is moderate, there is mild hostility. When minimal, there is peace, and one draws nearer to unity.

From these postures arise the two dominant ways of seeing the world—the glass half-full, and the glass half-empty—which become dominant personality types:

The one who thinks yes-That (yes to God, or yes-whatever it may be) and feels drawn to it, moves toward That, affirms it, and places it above himself, setting himself aside. That may be another person, or something not yet reached: a goodness to attain, an idea, a dream, a distant aim. The I places itself in service, and often feels lacking—small, ignorant, humbled before That—and so becomes immediately bound by it. When he thinks of his goal, he feels uplifted; but when he looks at himself in light of That, he feels inadequate, aching to change, to grow, to become worthy. He anchors his action in duty—in what he must still become to reach That shining perfection. His action is no longer free, for it orbits That which he has exalted. And yet, he seeks the joy and peace of others, inspiring all who come near with the fire he once lit in That, and now casts into each of Those who approach, so they too may love with the same sacred longing. He does what God, or the beloved, asks of him—because he loves. This is the way of devotion, the way of Christ.

The one who thinks no-That (no to God, or no-whatever it may be) and feels aversion, turns away from That, denies it, steps ahead of it, leaving it behind as illusion. He believes himself to be different, even though he can never truly part from objects, nor be entirely alone. He feels good in contrast to That; when he thinks of himself, he feels justified, strong. But when he turns his thoughts to That, discomfort arises, and he longs to change it. Yet he cannot, for the object will always differ from the subjet—it is what defines the I by distinction. In doing so, he begins to objectify even the self that distinguishes, until he edges toward the denial of the self altogether. This person roots his actions in will. He does what he wishes with

That from which he has separated, liberated, detached. He follows his own judgment first, always. And he reminds others of the pain that comes from unrestrained freedom, warning them of its cost. He points out the illusions in which they dwell and speaks of their duty to awaken—offering them his flawless method, the path he believes they must walk. This is the way of reason, the way of the Buddha.

The two extremes—one who abides in the Whole, and one who dwells in the Emptiness—ultimately arrive at the same threshold. For both dissolve into what lies beyond themselves. So it is that freedom leans toward the limit, and the limit opens into freedom. Each is folded within the other. From these movements of distinction and division arise all human discourses and dilemmas. And by simply listening to what we proclaim, to what we demand, we may glimpse the shape of the self we have chosen to become.

In practice, each time I adopt a verb and wish to develop it with another person, I must take into account its two faces. And when I contemplate these opposites, I find that: every time I think too well of someone, that person will feel bad about themselves; every time I think too badly, that person will feel good about themselves; every time I feel or think well of myself, there will be someone who feels or thinks poorly of me; and every time I think or feel poorly about myself, surely I will find someone who feels or thinks well of me. Said this way, it seems a labyrinth with no exit, but the good and bad we speak of always refer to a particular chosen verb, and above all, must be understood in terms of degrees of intensity. Primarily, "good" is the direction we move toward, and "bad" what we move away from—and these directions of movement can arise in varying amplitudes, for they are energy. To every degree of attraction corresponds a certain degree of aversion. If there is excess on one side, it is because something is lacking on the other.

We can verify this each time we shift the focus of our thought. If I am thinking about myself, I will feel one of the two forces; and if I wish, I have the possibility to turn toward the second and third person, and so begin to feel and think the opposite. Like when I desire something by thinking of an object, and then, turning to think of myself, I feel fear of losing it or powerlessness to retain it. Thus the verb turns.

From lesser to greater intensity, the pairs of opposites would be: delight–peace, curiosity–shame, joy–sadness, pride–envy, anxiety–annoyance, excitement–anger, desire–fear, obsession–desperation, vice–pain.

We ought to replace, for better understanding, the words "good" and "bad" with the corresponding pairs—so that when I say another feels bad when I think well of them, we keep in mind the degree of intensity. If I hold pleasant thoughts toward another person, I will generate in them a sense of calm and serenity, for the first pair of opposites is delight and peace. But if I flood them with praise and begin to share intimacies, they will begin to feel uncomfortable, and later self-conscious. And if I go too far, if I become excited, they will surely start to grow irritated—especially when I begin to demand all that they would now have to do. We will awaken in them the fear of being dragged into our delirium. And so on, and so forth.

When someone laughs, there is always sorrow hidden inside. We laugh at the clumsiness of another, which is also their pain. But it is not only theirs; soon it becomes ours. Every posture I take calls forth its opposite, following me like a shadow. Even if I destroy the person who embodies the contradiction, the contradiction itself simply finds another form. This world is transient, and it must be taken as such.

Let us now turn inward, toward the elements that compose us and that echo throughout the world: thought – (senses) – feeling; denial – (neutrality) – affirmation; subject – (instrument) – object. These are the primary threads in the weave of human being.

The contact between consciousness and force, and their

concentration, create the rhythmic movement of the Verb, which brings about lights and shadows, and the material world that is seen from a subject. Thus, we will find these particles wherever we are; there will always be first a thought, a feeling, and a movement—positive, negative, and shadowed—and then three persons in the environment (he/she, you, and I). Each pair, with its midpoint, in its own degree and cycle, combines to give us form. The common point goes from one to the other and relates both opposites; this word is spoken each time thought turns back toward the feeling that captivates it, in this way circling backwards. By turning over that particularity, one gives it a name and incarnates oneself into a three-dimensional body that holds that feeling in balance within; in one's heart that beats for That, and looks with curiosity at all the other sides that were left out and now make up one's new human scene—for through that choice, one has lost sight of the original movement. This is why the Verb must return him to that origin later, through being chosen—meaning, first transforming him into the suffering object of that choice; thus, the one who loves will be loved, the one who hates will be hated; and never strictly by the same object.

When one loses sight of the whole and the rhythm that flows through it, one clings to a few particles, identifying with some and casting the others out. These abandoned sides will then rise up from the outer world, calling us to remember.

In the sphere's diagram, we see these elemental presences ordered. We can glimpse which qualities we've taken as our own to relate to That, and also which remain for That to relate to us. For if one path is taken, That must momentarily flow through another. Or put another way, when we bind ourselves to any three terms, we form a new particle—an atom of matter—and its reflection in anti-matter. This is why it is said: there is no sound unless someone hears it. Just as there is no speaking without listening, no seeing without being seen, no loving without being loved, no guiding without being guided.

If I feel pain, someone will think the thought that heals. But if I think only of the great good I can take, someone—who embodies the place from which that good was drawn—will feel sorrow. If I dream of building pyramids, millions will be enslaved, and their suffering will call forth someone who dreams of my downfall. Thus will I also feel sorrow in time. So are formed the pairs of sensations we've already named—speaking and listening, doing and resting, delighting and surrendering, laughing and weeping, fullness and effort. These alternate, turning in cycles.

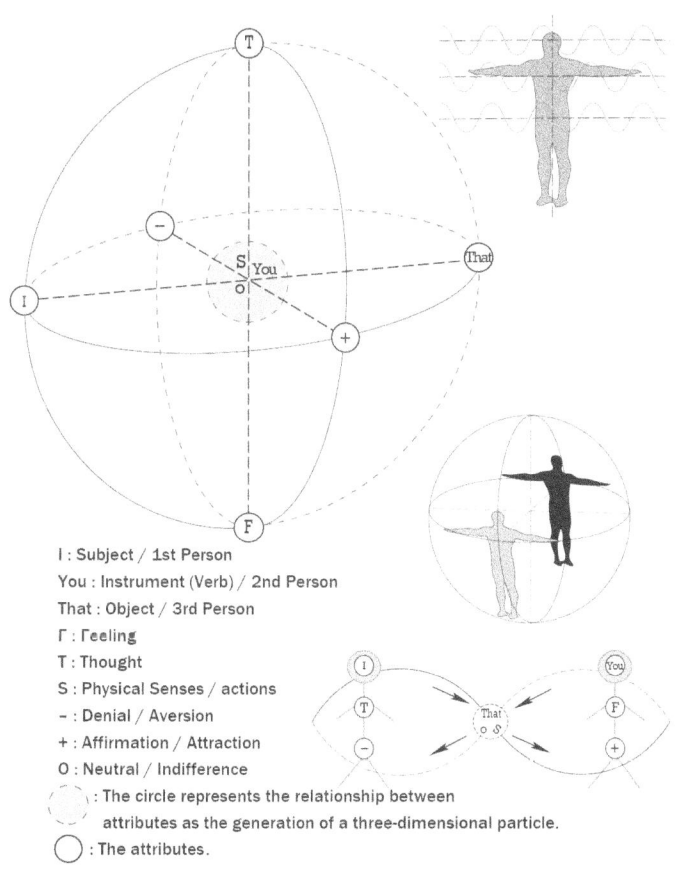

I : Subject / 1st Person
You : Instrument (Verb) / 2nd Person
That : Object / 3rd Person
F : Feeling
T : Thought
S : Physical Senses / actions
− : Denial / Aversion
+ : Affirmation / Attraction
O : Neutral / Indifference
⌢⌣ : The circle represents the relationship between attributes as the generation of a three-dimensional particle.
◯ : The attributes.

When the "I" is a hidden interior known only to itself, and objects too carry unseen leanings, we encounter a threefold unknown, an inner dimension of three more, and a shared communion with three again. So when two of us confront each other, and one lays claim to three of these elements, leaving none for the other to join in, the only role left for the second is to embody the remaining three. From this we come to see: to bring forth a positive response from the world outside, it is enough to let go of the "I." To empty ourselves, to serve, to yield in favor of the other. In this emptying, we nourish the outer world. The tree, well-tended, bears fruit. And if we feel ignorant, we draw near something that thinks and feels kindly toward us, something that wishes to protect.

One might think: why not just reach out and take what is good, without work, without sacrifice, without denial? And yes, that is possible. Some live by this rule. But when we grasp at the positive first, the negative soon follows. And if the good we claimed was not truly ours, then we have not only gained a prize—we have made an enemy, waiting in silence to strike back. That energy will find form through someone, somewhere. All flee the greedy one. To be hated, it is enough to hunger only for one's own gain.

Likewise, when we think of the wonder of That, we may give rise to someone who turns away from themselves entirely—like the worshipped artist who ends in madness or vanishes into death. Still, we cannot cease thinking of the good, for it is the river's course, the natural motion toward light. But we can resist throwing ourselves into it wildly. We need not cling. That which is truly good will arrive, will blossom, and will pass. We must not seize it, swell it, follow it everywhere, until it fails us and turns bitter. That is why we are told: only God is truly good. Seen this way, we begin to notice that the world flows within us, always shifting. And the unknown opens wide before our feet.

Likewise, the best thing one can do to lessen the painful

distances of affirmations—which are what cause us suffering—is to identify, in every situation that affects me, where each of these elements is located: with which I identify, and with which That observes me. By knowing the present and the past of my relationship with That, I can easily foresee the future. Put another way: when I know my interior and recognize the shared points, the remaining elements through which the other sees me can be inferred—those that will later be mine to look through, in some other moment. Thus, in this back-and-forth, we pass these shared points between us like a ball. When the ball reaches us, through what we do, say, and desire, we change its charge and throw it to the other side. And so, the other responds to that charge of ours with a new one. But life is not a ball game—no one wins in life. Whoever believes they've won something is already in the process of losing it. Existence is a perfect balance; there are no gains, no losses. And so, when we carry our situations with peace, and they become pleasant, we move naturally toward union.

Mutations:

The four postures mentioned earlier are mirrored in nature by the four seasons of the year. Each season corresponds to fire, sky, water, or earth—just as shown by the sages of the East in the "Book of Changes". And each of these seasons divides again, according to whether it is in its time of rise or of decline. This further division arises because each of the four elements forms for itself a closed, cyclical body—a living being that breathes these movements. The four elements, through differentiation, generate within themselves a being that watches them from a distance. This being seems to make use of them, yet in essence, it is the very instrument the elements use to transform their world. The inner and outer aspects of the elements can be distilled into eight stages or subdivisions—steps through which each movement of our nature unfolds. These stages are felt even when we take a sip of water, and they are reflected in different kinds of personalities.

Each person will identify with, or adopt, one of these eight postures, and move among the other seven until a new mutation occurs. Each posture plays a role, carries a specific quality, and serves its function so that the movement may be fulfilled. These qualities and functions are thoroughly described in the "Book of Changes"; our reading here will focus on tendencies of behavior in the human being. What we call "I" is the subject, the substratum, pure awareness. And what we call "That" refers, before all else, to the totality of objects, along with all emotions and thoughts that, in their offering, spill forth before our stunned "I." Depending on how we look upon that totality, it takes form—it becomes something objective, real—something that confronts us and fills our life with meaning and direction.

Each of us adopts a preferred "That." And though at first it may seem we are the ones chosen by the world, both "I" and "That" emerge in the Verb, in a circular movement that, depending on how one looks, either moves outward or returns. This rhythm of human nature is the same for me and for all the "Thats," whether chosen or not. The variable that determines our experience before life is the range of our obstinate free will toward the objects; and transcendence is the consciousness of unity.

Let us begin in the full darkness of the unknown and unmoving, with its following qualities:
—In thought: ignorance or negation
—In the body: the subject, the I
—In feeling: concentration or aversion.

A cold, deathly breath paralyzes the soul. We become aware of the banality of our life. This form represents surrender in movement. It is the one who completely denies itself, the one who receives the meaning of movement in its purity, without any personal point of view to modify, repress, or accelerate it. The receptive surrenders so that the movement may unfold before it; it is the space where the action takes place, where sound resounds, where destiny expresses itself. Everything is made for that silent emptiness of self, for the I is in reality only that emptiness, which—depending on its concentration—allows for a specific development of the Whole, of a That. The intensity of the negation will be given by remaining too

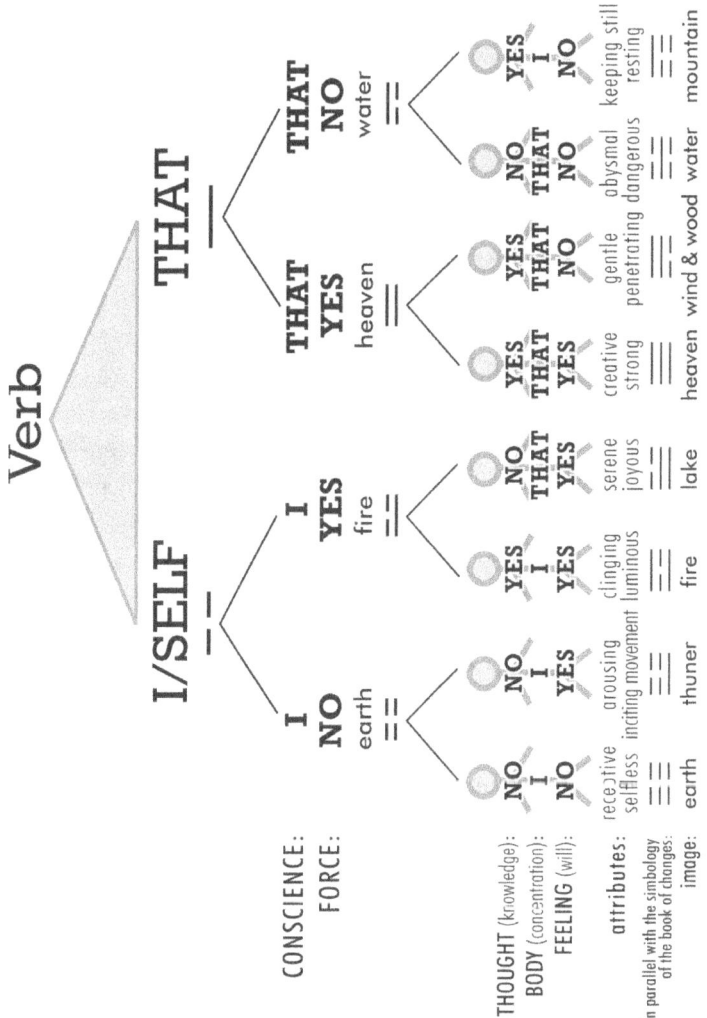

long locked within one's own ignorance and insisting on that posture; this will generate not recognizing oneself, not loving, not being able, not knowing how to do anything well. And this constant surrender to inertia will make us feel frustrated, used, drained, sad, fearful, and filled with self-destructive thoughts. If the intensity of the negation increases, the person will sink into some kind of incessant movement of escapism in which they will lose and dissolve themselves—a suicide that may or may not be conscious: "Others seem so intelligent beside us," life seems to have no meaning, we no longer recognize anything valid in ourselves, we find no understanding. Yet it is precisely because of this surrender that movement may finally unfold fully and reveal its truth in a new knowing—like when, only after exhaling everything, we are finally able to inhale and fill ourselves with fresh air. In a lighter intensity, one may renounce their passions and surrender peacefully to the silent uncertainty of the unknown, like in a deep sleep—after having previously given all our energies to That. Its quality is to be selfless, and its image is the Earth.

Within the very heart of darkness, light is hidden—spirit enclosed within matter. Thus, the excessive concentration collapses, scattering its particles in rebellious frictions that burst forth, giving way to the light of a new star, a new day. Stillness hides and concentrates the leap into movement; a leap achieved by what it once sowed in its dreaming womb, born from unfulfilled desires—then it begins to express. This gives rise to the second form or stage, which represents that which moves, that which stirs:

—In thought: ignorance or negation
—In the body: the subject, the I
—In feeling: expansion or attraction

Without knowing how, one finds oneself before an explosive well-being—and its image is thunder. There is no knowledge, but a force propels one into movement, like a thirst that ignites, and one does not know what to do.

Thus begins the search. The force pushes, groping for a way out, like a seed. If one remains stubborn in this posture, all one achieves is the denial of a force that begins to accumulate and will drag us outward, like a newborn being delivered. This can give rise to uncertainty, clumsiness, even injury—acting impulsively under the pressure of thought repressing a growing force, which will manifest as a thunderbolt crashing at our feet, awakening and stirring the dormant seed from its slumber. In its gentler form, it is when we feel well without being the cause—simply enjoying ourselves for being alive, loving our curious imperfections, even feeling at ease and well cared for in our ignorance, like children. As our excitement grows, we might even laugh at how poorly we do things—delighted by the commotion we cause. But in greater intensity, this force tends to spill into places it ought not to reach.

Now this pleasant feeling, this acquired force, displaces ignorance by drawing into thought all our possibilities, thus generating an idea to guide and direct it. This is the third stage: the person who affirms himself from a place of well-being.

—In thought: knowledge or affirmation

—In the body: the subject, the I

—In feeling: expansion or attraction

When lightning strikes the earth, fire is born—luminous and clinging. In the simple case of drinking water: he already knows that what he desires is water, and knows where he will draw it from. Now he sees he can carry out his will, for all the conditions are in place. But if one persists in this state, a herd of pride will drive him to the summit of imbalance, where nothing dares to truly touch him, fearing to be consumed by the flames of his arbitrariness. For fire burns by devouring the earth that feeds it, and the subject burns with the passion of his reference, from which identity draws its nourishment—devouring all in the name of thirst, or whatever he considers his idea, power, wealth, or desire. At its gentlest, this is the fascination with oneself—brimming with life and vigor in search of the highest possibilities. The "I" that truly advances is the one that ceases to think only of itself, and instead considers That, dedicating itself to the healing of what lies beneath. For this reason, living in balance with the opposite is the foundation of a healthy life. And so, in the next state, since the I now holds full affirmation, it will inevitably encounter the negation of That.

Fire in motion encounters water at rest. When it turns its gaze toward the other side, it sees itself reflected in the lake. Thus is born the fourth stage:

—In thought: ignorance or negation
—In the body: That, the object
—In feeling: attraction or expansion

Its attention is placed on That, as upon an unknown path waiting to be explored; like the veil of a curtain we long to pull aside, like something that must be changed—trial and error. Immediately after reflecting on how good one feels and what one is capable of, thought turns to all that must be altered to reshape That according to desire. In the case of drinking water, this would be going to the river, turning on the tap, or searching for a glass. With cheer, one feels drawn to fix what appears broken or less than ideal. This gives the stage its quality: the delight of adventure. For That, which does not align with one's ideals, does not disrupt the well-being. Instead, it draws the gaze with fascination—distance becomes magnet, and the very possibility of changing it becomes an irresistible lure, like an inventor with his creation, or a father gently correcting his child. But if one persists too stubbornly in a possessive mood, the delight turns sour. A taste develops for expanding upon imperfections, for seizing on small misfortunes with mockery or abuse. Worse still is the one who approaches That only to harm it—he digs deeper into his own misfortune, intensifying the very imbalance that returns him to the prior stage, unwilling to move forward. Only when one's inner well-being becomes capable of nourishing That—filling its lack, restoring balance—does the movement continue, to the benefit of both.

Taking the effort to modify the environment produces effects. In this way, the person may finally find the water and drink it, or encounter the consequence, the meaning, the solution, the love. The subject makes direct contact with the object and truly comes to know it. That surprises us with something unexpected and delightful—like Newton's apple, which through a blend of effort, faith, and providence, finally reveals itself and brings satisfaction. At first, the link between a movement—a verb—and the effect it produces takes us by surprise. But with repetition, we refine it, we practice, and we begin to master it. The transparency of the lake reflects the sky, giving rise to a broader comprehension, a new point of view. This is, in itself, a creative act—as the quality of this stage reveals—and its image is the sky, the most powerful:

—In thought: knowledge or affirmation

—In the body: the object, That

—In feeling: expansion or attraction

In this phase, a truth is established—what is right, what is meaningful, what stands out from the whole, even the god to follow. It becomes the point of support, the seed of the next movement once the current one completes its cycle. Thus, our next life will unfold within the landscapes imagined during this one, just as this one grew from what was loved in the last. By this logic, we become That which we once loved. And in so doing, we evolve. We choose effects, shape the world, and from that experience, build the next—until we finally transcend ourselves.

Now, just as a painter, having finished his final brushstroke, steps back to contemplate his work from different angles; or as the musician listens to his composition, seated calmly, from the outside or in its recorded echo; or like the builder who, after completing his structure, watches it fulfill its purpose to perfection—so too, one continues to affirm That in thought, yet begins to take distance. At first, this withdrawal is gentle, meant to gain perspective—to see it from where it all began, from the I. He remains at a distance and observes, offering praise. Thus, affirming That passively, he begins to influence others softly, without friction or force, indirectly, for he is the one stepping back. He grows distant from That, sensing it slipping away or being left behind, all while showering it with praises and longing for others to behold it too. Then arises the wish to share with others the newfound knowledge he has received. The quality of this stage is what is soft, what penetrates:

    —In thought: knowledge or affirmation

    —In the body: the object, That

    —In feeling: concentration or aversion

He affirms That from the serenity of retreat, and its image is the wind, gently pouring the light of heaven into the grain of wood. We have the water, but our thirst now quenched, we begin to feel full—and we see that it is best to pass the water on, for another to drink. To stubbornly linger in this stage can result in a kind of ideal for which one consents to suffer—like one who gazes long at what once was good, which now can no longer be, which moves away, while he remains fixed at the horizon, waiting for That to return at any moment... or believing it might be seized by force.

Still, the day will come when one turns around and accepts that That has already been enough; and since he no longer truly needs it, he lets it go. Yet worse off is the one who cannot stop smoking, or eating, or earning—those things he enjoys but which, in excess, now cause him harm. Greed turns That, once sweet, into poison. Then suddenly, its limitation appears, perhaps through misfortune, perhaps through illness. But if one remains measured, thought softens the separation. In the absence of That, one may see: it is not needed right now. We must learn to let the water pass without fearing we may never drink again. When one needs something too much, and grows dependent, a moment always comes when That, which once brought joy, now feels burdensome—and begins to do the opposite. This can plunge one into the depths, where rage rises and may become dangerous. This is the quality of this stage:

—In thought: ignorance or negation
—In the body: the object, That
—In feeling: concentration or aversion

That was enough—no more of That for now; he must return to himself. Yet at times he even longs to flee from what the excess and dependence on That bring about in him, drifting from his fortune like moving water that seeks a place to rest, entering, filling, and eroding every hollow, opening a path through the stones. An exaggeration at this stage will lead to a personality in conflict with the outside, faced with what his vitiated preference has achieved, and he will wear himself out uselessly, fleeing his destiny and fighting against the flaw in That which causes him so much fear and repulsion. At a lesser intensity it will grant him a certain calm in action, for he moves among things without clinging to any; he simply lets them pass, assigning little importance or reality to this passing. Calmly—at most, slightly weighed down—he will merely regard That as having fulfilled its purpose. If it does not turn out as before, it is because at this moment it is unnecessary, and a certain balance must be met for a former fire that burned immoderately.

But once he thinks of the absence of That, he instantly begins to recall how he enjoyed it, how good it was for others, and even how to obtain more. He reflects on the knowledge he holds and how important he believes he is, resting in the calm of his past adventures. Until it happens that the goodness he believes himself to possess is not enough—neither to feel complete nor to attain That which he so deeply desired. This confuses him and leads to reflection, giving rise to stillness, the quality of this stage:

—In thought: knowledge or affirmation
—In the body: the subject, the I
—In feeling: concentration or aversion

He affirms himself from the serenity of rest. The best moments return to his memory, like an elder or an ill person remembering how good they once were. Water can rest peacefully in the depressions of the earth carved by mountains; these mountains are the image of this stage. The I turns inward once That, for better or worse, has passed. In a mild intensity, he feels at peace with himself, daydreaming of what he would do if he could, letting his passions roam freely in the brief theatre of imagination. But if he clings too strongly to this posture, he will feel painfully disappointed in the impotence of his good intentions—and more intensely, he will only deceive and harm himself by believing he can, when in truth he lacks the strength. In any case, those affirmations, those dreams, were themselves a limitation, leading him back to self-denial, for the thirst is no longer there. The mountain of affirmations returns to its elemental origin: the Earth. We are drawn inward, into pure receptive awareness, into a momentary stillness—for the earth will cradle us like new seeds, allowing us to rise again in the time and space of the creative, to begin a new cycle of movement.

We all pass through these stages of movement born from our contact with nature. And as we identify with or surrender to certain inclinations or attitudes, we generate effects upon the world around us—thus, we will also encounter any of these same attitudes reflected in the external. From this, sixty-four possibilities arise: combinations even more defined, more clearly outlined.

(It is recommended to do a second reading substituting the word "That", for what worries on or draws one's attention).

– consequence –

The experience

All of us, at some point, feel an intense and persistent yearning for peace and plenitude. We seek to understand what is happening to us and to the world, and so we cling to ideas, to circumstances, to people, investing all our faith in them. Yet all these efforts seem to lead nowhere essential. Again and again, we return to an involuntary end, a dead end, left bewildered and uncertain about how to continue. Our inquiry is followed by a deep unease.

A dark abyss opens before us. There is no light to explain why we are alive. All that we had once held as real is revealed as self-deception. We had been living outside of reality and yet we lived; and now, not even reality itself seems real. Everything becomes a mirage of our own invention. How can I go on existing without knowing anything essential about this very existence? We're not even certain of the ground beneath our feet. We only wish to escape, to wake from this dreadful illusion.

This period of incubation is the prelude to a final catastrophe. All that remains is to throw ourselves into the void, to surrender to fate. And according to that illusion—our self-deception—the Unknown will respond with a new truth. When the will to live finally crumbles, and thought lays down its certainties, a quiet purification arises—opening the space for the gaze to rest upon the essence, which is the spirit.

In nature, we see this same impulse: the search for light, growth, blossoming, and bursting. Then suddenly, the truth takes its place. Wherever we are, it appears. And God overwhelms us with its magnificence.

At first, the conclusion "I am the whole" seems absurd. How could I be the stone or the flower in my hand? I am the one holding it. But the stone is, the flower is, and so am I. The fact of being is natural. There is no problem there, no desire. When we surrender, we may enter a subtle state of peace and contemplation, where the boundaries between object and self begin to soften, and if we remain in that fullness, gently, like a breath, those boundaries vanish.

The dimensions of reality open into new sights. They crisscross, merge, interpenetrate. I can no longer say that what I see is not me. Immersed in this experience, our human body vanishes—we try to look for it, and find only a unified whole, where ordinary objects are no longer there. And yet, despite the transformation, we are still here. We become the mind that penetrates all things—a stream of boundless potentialities, shifting and flowing in a new dimension, without our consciousness being altered or disturbed in the least. And we contemplate the infinite and its power of possibilities.

In that space, I could manifest anything just by thinking it. Reality shifts like a dream; it is only mind. Everything is thought. And then terror rises, the abyss yawns open before our newborn understanding. Like infants entering the world, we cry out. In the depths of the absolute, we are terrified by what might happen—though it already has. And grasping for what we know, we return to the world of forms. But now, renewed. Transformed. This experience of unity—of being beyond the three-dimensional body, beyond death—is what confirms the existence of the divine. In that moment, the first words to emerge from illumination are: "I am the whole." The personality loosens its grip. It dissolves into something beyond words. Into an order utterly other than the conventional. If such an experience did not exist to confirm the claim, the claim itself would be utterly false—and it would not have endured.

Through this Tao, Logos, Prana, Holy Spirit, Nirvana—call it what you will—we come to know that death is not the end. But neither is the world, not as we once knew it. We stand within a new dimension of thought. There is no up, no down. No inside, no outside. We can travel to other times, enter the minds of others, know their thoughts, see through their eyes. But even these wonders fade in comparison to the unfolding kaleidoscopic dimensions of the Whole.

We are space and time unbound—what more could we possibly need? That the experience not slip away, of course. But still, it is brief, arriving only when it wills.

The greatest tragedy is how much we love the world. Rather than move beyond it, we turn back toward what we desired from it. And so, we are returned to it. No longer with special powers, only with what is necessary. Usually, that means compassion. But the gate is closed. The experience cannot be accessed at will. And now we must suffer again—without reason, simply by choice.

Still, the vision remains. It reveals the ocean from which all rivers flow and to which all return. We can no longer be fooled about what is truly important. Reality, we discover, has nothing to do with what we once called real. There are levels within matter, layers of truth. We cannot fall into saying that the contemplation of unity is real while ordinary experience is mere illusion; the ordinary body is like the boat we use to cross the river—once we reach the other shore, it is no longer useful for moving forward, and we must leave it behind.

The subtle world does not negate the dense—it justifies it, refines it, even as objects lose their former value. That is

– Derivative 1 –

Love, Passion, and Commitment

The search for truth seems to begin in two ways.

One arises when, having all I need and want, I still feel an emptiness—a quiet ache for something deeper, a meaning that eludes. The other, more common, begins when that which we truly love turns away with cold indifference.

How is one to accept a world where love goes unanswered? The only answer, perhaps, is this: the one we love may have little to do with the love we feel. For love is not born from another—it is the recognition of unity, a silent empathy that draws us toward what we already carry within. It may be revealed through a person,

but it is not the person who causes the love.

It is true that the feeling of love always appears tied to a specific place, involving a particular object—be it a person, an animal, nature, a gleaming stone, or a higher experience—but it is not the object or place that holds the power to summon the feeling of union. If it were, it could do so with anyone, and with us, at any time. But we see this is not so. In fact, that very same object may eventually cause us the deepest suffering.

When all the love we feel for another lives within ourselves, the other can only witness it from outside, like watching a fire from beyond the glass. Only when the beloved draws near the lover through some shared action, some mutual breath, do the roles begin to shift—and in that exchange, the love may begin to be felt by the other too. It must be a back and forth, a gentle rhythm of giving and receiving, for us to slowly move closer to the mystery of union.

Even if we remain unaware in the play of love, the unity is always there, unshaken by the object chosen, unmoved by distance, unharmed by what the other may do. Love is the unity of all things, the only permanence.

Objects are but its shifting tides, its ever-changing dance through form and name. To rediscover love, the unity within all that is, which is God, is the soul's deepest purpose, its quiet return to the source.

Anything, or anyone, that awakens within us, even for a fleeting moment, the quiet bliss of being fulfilled, becomes our beloved. That instant of peace, where something enchanted us so wholly we forgot ourselves in it, can become the seed of a long journey: a thousand acts, a thousand sacrifices just to hold on to what once made us whole. We love another, truthfully, for the joy they once sparked in us, because they remind us of that moment when we were truly happy. And so, we identify with them, and delight in them all the more.

It is here that we often slip—when love transforms into passion: a highly personal and subjective form that shifts moment by moment. If only we had the strength to resist chasing those moments of enchantment, they would multiply, becoming more varied and continuous.

So we see: whenever we hold an idea of how love should be, we are no longer in love—we are in passion. The passionate attachment we feel is merely the desire for love—or rather, it is love confined into roles: lover and beloved, so that they might dance and ultimately merge.

The happiness found with another cannot guarantee a lasting relationship. There must be a balance—a mutual alternation between lover and beloved, a tending to the wounds and opposition that arise. In the end, the way you love the one you chose will determine your destiny. If you scorn the one who loves you, God will turn His face when you need Him most. If you lie to them, He will hide the truth from you, and you will live in fear and darkness. Imagine, then, what happens if you strike them.

It is impossible to be loved in return when one always plays the lover and the other the beloved. The beloved cannot love us back while they remain in the role of beloved—until the roles are reversed. If one insists on being the lover always, then when the other wishes to love, they must seek someone receptive. And those who always want to be adored risk complete dissatisfaction, believing they love nothing.

When love is returned, it becomes a dance, a sacred rhythm that draws lover and beloved into an embrace so deep that all boundaries dissolve. Back and forth, they move, until in the stillness between them, a new being is born, greater than either alone. But if we were to love God, then no person, no object would remain, only the radiant, boundless silence of the Infinite. And in that pure, ungraspable vastness, we might tremble. To be fully immersed in such overwhelming presence is to face the ancient fear the scriptures speak of, the holy dread that makes us long again for the safety of our smallness.

Marriage celebrates the mysterious union of two into one. A child is not only the continuation of life but the eternal testimony of their union; even if they part, the child will forever be the bond between them.

We make vows because unity has made us a new being—greater, safer, happier—and so we commit to the dance that seeks that happiness. And so, when the enchantment fades and flaws surface, when the price of passion is due, we might endure suffering together and reach a new joy.

If we are to live with another, we must first be clear: plenitude cannot come from the other, nor from their actions, nor from our expectations. If unity is based on expectations, the relationship is bound to fail.

We can inspire pleasure and joy, but no one can grant or take away another's fullness. Happiness appears naturally between us—it cannot be demanded. There must be mutual adaptability, a harmonic dance. I take a step, and the other does too—but not the step I want them to take, for that is my step, not theirs. The other behaves a certain way because they cannot behave otherwise. If I ask them to change so I may feel satisfied, they can ask the same of me—and that will never bring us together.

When we look at the blue sky, the stars, the horizon, the mountains; when we hear the birds or play with children, we make no demands—we are naturally joyful with them. We don't ask the sky to be green. If these things do nothing special to please us, and yet we feel content, it is because we accept them as they are. Nature gently awakens us from the bitter, restless self we seem to have become. In nature we are one with the moment, flowing with a world that does nothing in particular to please us—and yet we are at peace.

Our desire for fulfillment is but the echo of past joys come to visit. There is nothing wrong in them—until we chase them, mistaking them for love, forgetting that love has always lived within.

At times, it seems we love the longing more than the thing we long for. That feeling, born of distance, shifts when space narrows or grows. Draw too near or drift too far, and the passion may vanish, like mist touched by sunlight. But love is infinite and vast. It is the unity beneath all things. It does not vanish. It simply changes its form. It is ungraspable, and yet, it is never, ever lost.

- derivative 11 -

Beggar, King, and Sage

All eat and are eaten, all take and give. Kings are kings because, no matter what they do, that very thing becomes the food of the poor. Therefore, rich is the one who has something to do, to show, and to give. And because there are many who desire what he does, his wealth grows both in popularity and in material abundance. He becomes rich because he transforms what he finds and returns it for the benefit of others. The king exists in the spirit, in the willingness to take responsibility for action; that is how results are granted to him. For this same reason, those who inherit or usurp wealth are often not true kings; though if many desire what they have taken, they may become kings of usurpers.

The truly poor, who possess nothing, have nothing to give, but also nothing to defend. Having nothing, nothing can be taken from them, and they simply sit and watch what the king does with such enthusiasm. In balance, the king—sumptuously overactive—and the beggar—abusively idle—are the extremes that shape the sage. They make sense in him only at first, but later he levels them, and the differences dissolve. Yet for life to unfold, some distance is needed for the social movement of various roles. The poor have nothing to give because they believe they can do or offer nothing; one could argue they have strength, reason, and help to give—but only someone who gives knows that. The poor truly experience the helplessness of existence, without clear direction or will; and that condition is essential to contemplate the universe that constantly surpasses us in its infinite purity. That is why the poor who live this way are the sages. But those who don't stop their thought in emptiness infer instead that they must have something, and thus conclude their lack. They even fear something is owed to them and missing, and because of that lack, they cannot find peace. These, thinking they have nothing to give, ask and take, and if they hoard what they manage to grab, they may become poor millionaires—constantly using their lives to want more and more ("I need, I need, I need"), and despite that, find nothing to give.

Within each of us lives the begging one, who calls out to that higher force which holds what he lacks. He refuses to act until someone or something gives him what he believes he needs, nor does he feel capable, because he sees no other path forward; he represents stillness. Yet within us also dwells the king, the richest in spirit, who believes in the truth of his own thoughts and feelings, and tends to act upon the tasks that arise. He even presumes at times to be the benefactor of others. The king is movement, action; he uses whatever is at hand, that alone is enough. Even in the most unlikely of places, he will find some object with which to think, to act, to do something.

The sage claims no ownership. He knows that ideas do not arise in a specific person, nor is any particular action caused by another. To him, all comes from God. People either claim or disown what is divine. One is born and dies without knowing why, or when such fate was willed; we sleep and wake outside of our human will, by the ongoing movement of nature. That is why, for the sage, life unfolds beyond any human will. The monk allows himself to be shaped by God, for he knows his own powerlessness before the universe. That attitude of surrender always brings new understanding. Action arises—he does not reject it but takes his place in its unfolding, moving with it, being one with it. Yet he does not claim the knowledge as his own, and thus, he is not a king. The sage needs nothing and has nothing of his own to give, for he takes nothing for himself. He is everything that surrounds him. Nothing can be lacking, nothing can be added. He is both the eater and the eaten. And to fulfill the purity of this vision, he must let go of his actions and even his points of view, releasing the experience entirely to its infinite destiny.

The monk cannot bear the king's vanity when he proclaims: "I truly want nothing; I act for my people. What would they do without me?" Some kings have claimed to act in the name of divine will, others in the name of higher beings, of the people, and so on. But they have never learned that we are all instruments of God—even the animals. In his hours of solitude, the king pleads for meaning. His supposed brilliance is such that he finds no rest, for he feels he must be responsible for everything, and he clings to defending it. Movement laments itself, unaware that it has claimed rights from nothing, seizing actions it believes to be its own. And in doing so, it may have harmed or abused others. That is why every king is accompanied by a sage or his likeness, someone who sustains him and offers clarity and lightness to his self-imposed burden. Just as every State needs its Church.

The Church of a given community is the essential roof that the doers—the rich—cannot rightfully deny. Any action undertaken disturbs the delicate balance of the surroundings, of the poor—those who have nothing, who wish to do nothing, and even less to work. They must endure the whims of the rich, who in their unmeasured enthusiasm have left them without natural resources: space, food, and water. If where once stood a fruit tree now stands a building, the owner of the building must give of its fruits to those who once ate from the tree before he arrived. Though this may seem like an arbitrary obligation, it is an important matter of harmony and natural order. If one link is cut without continuing the chain, eventually the whole building will collapse. Although the kings managed to convince many that their projects were useful—and so some of the less rich and not-so-poor joined them and changed things—the poorest are not persuaded, nor do they see the point. They prefer to drift in their carelessness, surrender to fate, and accept what comes or is given. In truth, the poor are the constant denial of God toward the extravagant schemes with which kings sweep up the people. And while the king too may deny, he always does so with a greater affirmation that leads to new action.

Since it is the rich who changed the environment, they must provide the poor with what is essential to life, if nature has disappeared or someone has claimed it—who knows by what excuse. We can say that what is essential is life itself, and life provides for itself. We find it in nature: in food, warmth, shelter. It even generates more life by itself, ever new, without our knowing how or why. Thus, the community creates this place called church, where the poor come seeking what is essential. For this very reason, the church should always be open: the night refuge for vagabonds and beggars, and the daytime refuge for those poor in love.

The festivals of the entire community would take place there, because in their deepest sense, what we celebrate is the loosening of roles, what we celebrate is unity. That is: we are all equal, all one thought and one feeling, seated at a single table. This would take place in the church, since the poor cannot travel far, and the rich know that even the poorest of all is found there. So, partly to share, partly to help, and partly out of vanity, they will give what they have, show what they do to those who ask and those who want to see and listen. Some will bring food, others drink, others will come for something to eat or drink. In this way, those who wish to give gather and distribute, like bread at the table; and those who need ask, and if there is something, it will be theirs.

At these feasts, after everyone has eaten from the same table, comes the time to join in joy. And this is achieved by knowing and feeling we are all united. If I were truly united with someone, I would have to be able to know their thoughts and feelings. Because of this uncertainty—not knowing what the one beside me thinks—we are gnawed by doubt and insecurity. So, for this special celebration, the "Name of God" was chosen. It will depend on the congregation or belief to which one belongs. At a certain moment of the feast, the whole community agrees to want to feel that unity, that all, that God. And to achieve this, they decided that to begin to know what the other thinks, we all start by thinking the same thing: the "Name of God."

In that moment, the whole community looks into each other's eyes and sees reflected in their companion their own thought: "God." The game, of course, is not to cheat, because if I do, I will only feel my own individuality, separated from that growing force. In this way, people loosen, I feel cared for and safe in my thought because I know I'm not alone—we all think "God" together. It could have been any other word or sound. We can observe similar effects at concerts or sports events. But in those cases, the benefit of unity is only for a few people, those toward whom the thought is directed (which is why it is wise not to give our energy to just any clown).

In the midst of this repetition of "the Word," the question arises: What is this word, this thought? That is why it is later said: God is Love. Thought is, ultimately, the sensation it evokes, and sensation translates into a feeling that we nurture and call love. This sensation cannot be concluded or defined; only through thought can we capture it in fragments and fixed moments, which cannot be extended. Feeling is a force in constant change, elusive to definitions. What I think: God, is what I feel: Love. Thought is shared and united, feeling is shared and united. In this way, all distances are overcome with cleverness, practicality, and logic.

This ritual is practiced in every feast, gathering, ceremony, or mass; in that place and that moment, all is everyone's.

Still, there will always be those who seek only personal gain, wanting something to enjoy at another time and place, with a different purpose. Why only now? Why only what's here, if God is everywhere? As long as we think of another place and desire something from it, there will be division and no possibility of plenitude. But if one simply doesn't wish to be at the feast, that is entirely possible. Trying to stop them would be a mistake too, since unity is always present, wherever we may be.

The priest is the one who distributes what the rich give, for he knows through confessions the needs of the poor. He then communicates them to the rich, or to those who feel like doing and create things. In this way, the rich entrust him with what they have to offer and are inspired to make new things to give. Requests and discontent spark new challenges. The sage neither gives nor takes. He knows the thought but attributes it neither to himself nor to others. Action, whatever it may be, belongs to itself and is common to the whole and to all. That a particular person expresses it does not mean it belongs to them, or that it is exclusive, or that they are to blame in the pessimistic sense. This can be demonstrated by holding back a certain thought—soon someone or something will express it for us. Likewise, he knows that feeling does not belong to him. It does not come from him or enter him provoked by others. Feeling is a force contracting or expanding for the sake of the ongoing movement in which all take part.

The monk asks: What is still and moves at once? You, the Verb, and I are all and nothing at once.

- Derivative III -

Father, Mother, and Son

*The man pursues the woman,
and thus she engenders the child.
The man emerges from the child,
then observes and moves toward the woman.
The man finds protection in the child, his origin.
The man sees the woman in everything;
she is his natural destiny.*

*The woman pursues the child,
and thus he engenders the man.
The woman emerges from the man,
then observes and moves toward the child.
The woman finds protection in the man, her origin.
The woman sees the child in everything;
he is her natural destiny.*

*The child pursues the father,
and thus he engenders the mother.
The child emerges from the mother,
then observes and moves toward the father.
The child finds protection in the mother, his origin.
The child sees the father in everything;
he is his natural destiny.*

The child is neutral, still undifferentiated, asexual. As the child grows, they begin to become either man or woman, but the pure child remains always within, in both man and woman.

Thus, the child-man, through his child side, chases the father, and through his man side, pursues the future woman. And the child-woman, through her child side, also chases the father, and through her woman side, chases the potential child.

Thought is the father, feeling is the mother, and matter—the forms in which we exist—is the child. This can also be read as: subject, instrument, object; as positive, neutral, negative; God the Creator, the human being, and Mother Nature; consciousness, existence, and bliss; Father, Son, and Holy Spirit; from one comes two, from two comes three, and from three, all things. Even atoms function in this way. In every such triad, the functions hold. The Trinity is most holy because it is everywhere.

Life can feel like a constant struggle between the interests of the child, the father, or the mother—seemingly opposed. Man must realize that to reach his natural destiny, the woman, he must first embrace the child and begin from him to arrive at her. The woman, who sees the child in all things, places her attention on him; without a child within the man, she would never notice him. Yet she also knows that to engender the child she desires, she needs the man, and must go to him and surrender to receive it. The child too, realizing that his desired destiny is the father, must go through the mother. He remains close to her, for in her dwells the father. The father always returns and keeps his gaze upon her; there is where the child will surely find him.

A man-child, where the child dominates, will be adored by many women—but he won't care. His gaze is fixed on the father, or on the figure he has assigned as such: his goal, his god. The love of those women won't interest him much; they will seem like distractions. He is the child who doesn't see that his father is with the woman he left behind. If the man dominates instead, he will be admired by children, which feels natural to him. What truly concerns him is the love of a woman, and his focus rests entirely on what emerges when he becomes one with her. Here the man is dominant, and the child is repressed, forgotten. And that is why the woman looks at this man and sees someone without a child—someone who doesn't know how to play. And she, above all else, chases the child. In this case, the man fails to see that the woman seeks the child in him, wants to see him playing with what he loves, doing what we do best. If she does not see that child, she will lose interest. She will likely fall for another, someone she sees working passionately on what fascinates him. After all, no matter how important the task, it's still just a child's game.

A woman-child, where the woman dominates, will suffer for wanting a child that meets all her dreams. And once she has the child, she will suffer again when he pays attention only to the father. She will only receive the child when he rests, or when he reaches the father and sees him doing everything for the mother. It may be that she fails to see the child in the man who loves her. But if she were patient and allowed the man to pursue her, once his desire is satisfied, the child would emerge—which is what she wants. If not, the man will likely lose her attention by failing to meet the needs of his inner child—not realizing that it is this very childishness the woman waits for, to turn him into a father. When the girl dominates, she will look for a teacher—a father figure—and may project this role onto a man, a god, or even an activity.

In balance, the child finds that the father he seeks is within himself. For the father seeks the mother, and the mother is found in the child, and the child is himself. The man who searches for the woman finds her in the child, and the child within himself. The woman who seeks the child finds the child in the man, and the man within herself.

Heaven planted its seed in the beloved earth, from where life was born and where it rises again to the sky. This current is the primal desire, the very engine of life. When the three converge...

I could turn and ask the child, with unwavering gaze and full attention: What are you looking at? Why do you trouble me so? Instantly, the child will seek refuge in the mother, turning to her for answers to the father's questions, and ask her with the same intensity: What are you looking at? What is it you want from me? The mother, to understand her desire for the child, must remember what drew her to the father. At that moment, she was with him, thinking of him, united with him—emotionally, psychically, physically. And so the mother turns to me for help with the child's question, and asks me in return: What did you see in me? Why did you chase me so? Then I turn once more toward the days of my childhood, searching for the origin of these desires and circumstances. But my childhood was born of another her, and she of another me... and so on...

And so the three of us stand, gazing at one another with question marks floating above our heads. And the only answer we find is this: we can turn in the other direction too.

The meaning of it all—of life—is a current in motion, flowing now this way, now that.

The man knows himself as son and as man, He does not know himself as woman—he must meet her, and learn from her.

The woman knows herself as girl and as woman, She does not know herself as man—she must meet him, and learn from him.

The child knows nothing yet; He emerges from the mother, and discovers the father. He must come to know them, and learn from them both.

The man wrestles between his God and his woman,
the woman between her God and her child,
and the child between his mother and his father.

- notes -

Journal of impressions

- 1991 -

From your gaze, my transparency was born;
from your smile, my wings;
and from the kiss—love,
and the miracle of being
the shimmering glow of illusion
that enters each morning
through the window of your celestial palace,
and with soft caresses of petals,
awakens you amid sweet melodies.

- 1993 -

He no longer knew whether the stars seemed beautiful to him, or just a stupid lie. So he chose to shelter his heart in that cave of panting arteries. Yet the softest caress undid him, sending his heart fleeing toward soaring dreams that always prove impossible. And so he remained in a corner, part of the lament. Had he been one more chosen to suffer the guilt of others?n Or was he, in fact, the guilty one? He might have been a vampire—to suck the life from people like him. Or the scent of a violin—to soften hearts like his. But truly, I am him. The one who doesn't fit. The one who hanged himself with his own veins and left his corpse adrift, waiting to be swallowed or rescued by his own lies—it made no difference. Still, one day, his heart will again escape that nothingness, and maybe his illusion will once more fall before another impossible suicide. Having completed another turn in ignorance, in drowned cries of anguish, another of his children will expire. One by one, they will die in each rotation, until one of them overcomes the need that terrifies them, and hurls himself from the carousel into the void—to learn to fly.

> Better to know how to wait, to meditate,
> and not be impulsive.
> As the master says—let it swell,
> then, with just a little prick...
> The right time, the perfect measure—
> like magical passes.

- 1994 -

To be or not to be, body or soul, good or bad, black or white, inside or outside, inside or outside or inside or outside inside outside inside outside inside outside inside outsideinsideoutsideinsideoutsideinn... ooorgaaa... smsss...

Freedom must, be letting our good and our bad make love. That's why the religious right away teaches us to give God all our goods and our ailments.

Individuality
eats away at our being,
and when it starts licking our heart,
we turn to that miraculous substance
in many shapes and colors:
pills, powders, herbs,
televisions, sex, idolatries,
institutions, people,
fads, competitions, etc.

And so,
the more we consume,
the more we lull
that docile individuality.
But the longer it sleeps,
the stronger it grows when it wakes,
and it wants more.

We could consume until we die,
and then the "I" would grow so strong
it would be born again in another body,
to go on consuming us.

If we transform reality
into what we believe reality is,
then each being would have a different one,
and there would be no common ground.

We wouldn't be able to communicate with anyone,
we'd only be speaking
to our own fantasy.

What's strange is that
no one truly knows reality.
Some believe one thing,
some another...

Are we living alone
in the fiction our mind creates?

Tonight I spent hours searching for her,
wandered through many places,
saw many people,
but she was only in my mind.

And if she was within me,
why was I searching outside?

To have her in my mind
doesn't mean she's in me.

And if I am not my mind,
then what am I?

Confusion came
when I realized that in the desire
I thought purest,
hid my most perverse one;
and in the most perverse,

I found the most spontaneous and pure.
Tranquility:
when I let my desires go.

The fiercest creature,
endowed with great claws,
is the one that lives with the most fear.
She is naturally the most cowardly.

The most vulnerable creature
is the bravest,
for she doesn't need
to defend herself so much
in the face of death.

Why do I think I don't need
what I know I do want?
It must be precisely because I think.
I believe my being got trapped in a thought.

And so, I keep wanting
what I'm constantly thinking I don't.

Just now,
I almost became sound...
but I was afraid.

I was beginning
to intuit how everything is,

why, with the vision, we must refine the world we live in, for ordinary experience is the same unity, only seen from a different angle, from afar.

To weave both experiences of oneself into relation brings balance— and makes us whole.

but at once I intellectualized it.
I wanted to find out
why we can't see our true self.

And before I could peek,
I sensed that to grasp infinity,
one must be completely empty.

But I am still full of things.
Like these thoughts, for instance.

When I search for truth,
illusion harasses me;
when I seek fleeting pleasures,
truth harasses me.

Is there nothing to seek?

I thought I had a hole in my pocket,
but it was only a pocket in the hole.

The answer to every question
is the same question.
And the question to this answer
is the same answer.

With that, we now have
three questions for three answers.

The senses are not doors to the outside.
They are only mirrors.

We are constantly seeing ourselves
and do not recognize it.

God is love,
but love "does not exist."
What a relief!

Still, without love,
this life wouldn't exist.

That is as far as reason can go.
What a relief!

We are only contours within God.
If we dissolve the contour, we return to Being God.
And that contour is our mind, our ends.
Our End.

- 1995 -

Coming down the mountain, on the way to the city, one hears the noise of men trying to change things—proud even of their grotesque and polluting constructions. Now I see the filth, and my distrust toward them grows. Could this very distrust be the same filth?

I think of the universe as the place I'm in now—there is nothing more. The universe is really what I can see and hear; what lies beyond is merely the explanation of why I see what I see. At this moment, there is no universe beyond this room, with this music; the rest is just a descriptive definition of this reality, of this place. So at all times I am before the whole universe, before God, and yet I don't see it—I see something else. I superimpose another reality on what I see; before seeing it fully, I reduce it to the place I am now: a room with music.

For the moment,
to get out of the way,
to every question,
you can answer:
"It is and it is not";
since they become synthesis
in the next experience.

We would have to learn to think
as if who's next to us could listen.

To sin is to justify oneself for existing.

Do what you desire
whatever it is.

Even though the free Being
is also free of desire,
everything is the same,
it holds no preferences.

Because it is free of them all.

It is essential
to forget the past,
the future
and the present.

...and we would no longer speak to each other, but exchange images. Having incorporated the third eye, which is a projector of three-dimensional images, just as once we incorporated the mouth, which projects sound.

- **1996** -

God plays at being me.
And I let Him play...
I contemplate Him...
I play along...

The final current pulls me, and I cling to this stone. The ocean is just ahead. So much path I have walked! And now, just like that—everything is left behind? The Whole is coming, but the way of form is fading. Is there nowhere else to go? Have we arrived? Is this even conceivable?

And now what? I can't go back—the path is already known, and it wouldn't be the same. Staying on the stone isn't an option either—that would be like becoming a ghost, neither one thing nor the other. Though I might stay a while. After all, it's the end of a path I finally fell in love with. It is our romanticism that makes us enter the ocean with such slowness…

Writing about you is limit you.
And even to myself.

The "YES" in the feeling,
and the "NO" in the mind.

Considering that the mouth speaks
what overflows from the heart,
this is the formula for beauty.

The existence manifests itself to appreciate itself.
God is so vain that what he likes the most
is to look at his image in the mirror.

Everything speaks of the same thing,
even though the same thing never repeats.

I don't do things
I do with things,
like flowing;
though I must admit,
most of the time they do me.

The self-imposed demand for truth
is the worst torture.
It leaves you
spinning on yourself.

Is the most real suffering physical,
emotional, or psychological?
Truth is, we all go through all three,
and each of us
believes our suffering is harder than anyone else's,
when all suffering is the same suffering.
By habit, we even enjoy provoking it in others,
becoming the very evil we once rejected.
The most unbearable thing
is having to endure advice from the ignorant.
So we persist in our pain,
and all that people hate and reject,
we will embrace in solitary, shadowed love,
for nothing must be left out,
and someone must stand in solidarity with them all.

One must keep in mind,
before climbing,
that at the summit
there is nothing
but the satisfaction of the journey.

The wisdom of the innocent
is coveted and envied.
That's why
they are treated like fools.

I side with no one,
and yet,
I love no one more.

The idea is born in unity,
develops,
and resolves in feeling.
The feeling is born from the idea,
develops,
and resolves in what is seen.
What I see is born of the force of feeling,
develops,
and resolves in what I think.
Thus arise a positive, a negative, and a neutral,
which will be resolved in the force that enacts them—
and so on again, and again...

The dreamed self,
when going to sleep,
dreams it is awake.

- **1997** —

I "are" everything

After defining that,
I return to myself,
and I define again,
and return again,
and so on...

Neither near nor far,
neither returning nor defining,
neither me nor that,
neither and nor again,
neither neither...

I am not God; I am what God wants to do.

I is a point in the view of anything.

Life is Yes is No is Yes is No is Yes is No is Yes is No is Yes is No is Yes is No is Yes is No is Yes is No is...

Some highlight the "is No", others the "is Yes". Others say: "No is Yes"; others: "Yes is No"; and others just "is..."

Truth is when I can't tell whether I'm exhaling, inhaling, or holding my breath.

Why not me? So that you yes. I no you yes Ino youyes I noyou yesI no youyes Ino you yes I no youyesInoyouyes In oh no you & I...

- 1998 -

I am the "I" of all things.
And only you, I see in them.
Where we both dance a unit called God.

When I want to write what I thought; misses the sense.

I seek the truth.
I write, as such, a longing.
Something spontaneous.
A I-don't-know-what.

I listen to music, follow the music,
write the listening and the singing;
full of pleasures and searching for something more.
Something more—her—not but... yes but...
now me and here, there...
unreal fantasies and important inert realities without them.
Questions—I can't find the question mark on this machine.
So many questions to ask—
why is there always something wrong?
Because of what I see, what I am,
because of justification, excuse, explanation,
wanting to know.
What can be known?
What is it that I know right now?
I listen. I see. I write.
Bored, it's the same—but no—
to ramble, to write the first thing that comes to me—
I don't know why—
simply because it came,
because I always ask why,
and invent an answer,
from which I then ask why again...
It seems endless torture,
but really it's silly.
He is... God... lights... shadows... shifting orders,
worlds within worlds,
poetry of being the same being...

I would like to fulfill all His desires,
then something new...
characters, stories of gods,
fantastic dimensions...
and the suffering within this reality,
and the why?

Of all the fantastic dimensions,
the one I most cherish in my heart is hers and mine.
Is there something wrong with me?
As long as I believe,
I'll see the edge, and the yearning to reach it…
Where do I want to go?
Nowhere.
Existence, sensations, thoughts—they're natural.
They arise…

- 1999 -

In the name of our blessed Emperor, all-knowing Lord of the middle sector, true maintainer of balance, I raise my voice in response to your request that we become each day more perfect.

Thus, the hand of my Lord is rich in ideas of order, and if your holy patronal trinity allows it, we shall plant, with the help of the mage, lord of the realm of fantasy, a palace of illusions that shall be a direct gateway to the sun.

There, in communion, shall gather the fruits of our four provinces: Reality, Illusion, Seeking, and Waiting. So that this small order may later allow us to continue sailing with passion through beloved chaos.

Though my Lord finds himself in dark hours, for his harvests have diminished, he gives thanks in this song that the territory of his temporal and spatial consciousness has been extended, and he reaffirms his throne by beautifying his kingdom.

May your holy trinity enlighten us all.

Ignorance before the infinite dominates us, the anguish of not knowing paralyzes us, and fantastic explanations arise to tell us why things happen.

But the sorrow remains and we are left standing—what can one do?

Only from the perspective of life does death exist, only from the perspective of success do failure and frustration arise; from God's perspective... everything returns to Him. What real danger or sorrow could we face?

Perhaps suffering, unconsciously, is a test—to see how far from God or happiness we can stray.

Apathy, weariness, frustration—they fill us with confusion, ignorance, emptiness (and we beg for a remote control). If we were to face suffering truly, from the root—that void, that senselessness, that violence—and finally give it the attention it's been crying out for, it would speak its truth, be satisfied, and make room for something else, another reality.

For in the end, those feelings of sadness are always the same: We grieve over death or deficiency, and we rejoice in life and the extraordinary.

Either we turn sadness into beauty—apply imagination and art to it so it feels heard and stops haunting us—or, once and for all exhausted by sorrow, we create new feelings: subtler, more perceptive, compassionate, empathetic.

I give shape to my sadness by asking myself: Why, if I love her, does she not love me? How can love be unrequited? Why couldn't we fall in love at first sight and be happy forever? Why isn't everything as magical and wondrous as I wish it to be?

By now I should have the audacity to consider my sadness magical and wondrous—this confusion, this fantasy, this unreality or disaster. Where did all of it really come from?

To get tangled in what happens to us is fantastic; the truth is, we don't know (we only speculate) anything at all about why things happen around us. At first glance, we might claim our lives are a nightmare, but things don't happen to be explained—they happen to be lived, matured, exhausted, transcended, cultivated, and so on…

The event itself is the most urgent thing. But I feel mad, obsessed, clumsy, anxious… How long will I keep asking, keep torturing myself? Happiness becomes such a costly thing—a heavy burden of unsatisfied and meaningless seeking.

The strange thing seems to be that even if we don't want it or know anything at all, plenitude is always present everywhere, available to whoever calls it. God is always here. That's why we take our time in returning to Him, and meanwhile, we play with whatever most draws our attention.

Just as there are people who enjoy horror movies, our true self is attracted to pain and sorrow. Whatever the case, it will, unconsciously, get involved in some situation that—sooner or later—makes it partake in that horror, in that sorrow.

Dreams only push us—they give us the initial nudge. Then life, so wonderful, immediately commits us violently or peacefully—or rather… may our dance flow through all things, caressing them like a soft breeze, bringing them all into this incredible gathering of magical worlds in which we move, full of the joy of being together, dwelling in the fullness of satisfaction with all that surrounds us.

The poet within us, upon the first impression of beauty, stamps his ideal and sets off in pursuit of it.

- 2000 -

Sometimes identity feels essential,
to identify oneself.
But with what or whom will I identify?
Yet I can be nothing more than myself.
I myself am identity.
To whom then shall I attribute myself?
...To God, to you, and to me.

Every time I do something, it feels like I'm wasting time, and yet not even seconds pass before the thought arises that something must be done. To act—out of fear of decay and destruction? Would it be better to simply do something, anything, so that if it goes wrong, it doesn't bother us?

But what is it that I'm really seeking in what I want to do? If happiness is everywhere, what sense does it make to do anything? Sense. To be. To feel is to do something—to think, to perceive, to contemplate...

The meaning of feeling is me, is you, and is for itself, and none of the three, or any one of them.

Enlightenment.   Mind—everywhere.   Indestructible. Joyful.

Neither to surrender
nor to dominate,
the transparent mind.

To know, one must first ignore;
and to ignore, one must first know.
Knowing this may be useful—
but it only makes us more ignorant.

You can fight to become a winner,
but at the end of triumph
you'll find the disappointment of the ephemeral.
Or you can be a loser,
and at the end of sorrow
find the relief of the same ephemeral.

Or you can be one of us—
and read us,
and think us…
and imagine us…

The only way to escape good and evil
is to offer goodness to God.
I don't win,
I don't lose.
I am the prize.

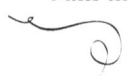

It is an art to present oneself to the unknown and to look at everyone as if for the first time, when attention becomes sharp because a mystery still holds the distance between both parties. We know we are different, and in that unknowing, we long and wait for anything to move—anything that might give cause for union or separation, for a shared knowledge, for the continuation of movement. We proceed like this until, suddenly, we realize we have no idea how we arrived at this exact place where we now stand.

We look around us, we know there is something... but we cannot define it. And if we wanted to go deeper in trying to define it, it turns out to be as vast and all-encompassing as there are worlds across the universe. One might even try to define the unknown as "vast and all-encompassing," as "looking around us," or even as "worlds across the universe"—infinite...

To realize that we don't know leads us into a new, purified form of knowing. But once we believe we have grasped it, the unknown reappears, stirring the thunder, raising the earth, and letting eternity blossom again in its full magnificence. In that moment, we find ourselves face to face with wonder, unable to explain anything—and so we give the experience a new name. A new knowledge has emerged, and a long list of rascals to claim it, a new challenge to master it and put it into effect, the same ever-present force in motion.

So, ultimately, neither knowledge nor ignorance holds absolute ground. What is, is not, it is, it is not, it is it is not I 0 I 0 I 0 I 0 I 0... Our role is to help whatever appears before us to blossom. Right and wrong do not exist in any fixed way—that is why, in the end, everything balances itself.

- 2001 -

As a child I played "neither yes, nor no, nor black, nor white." And when I didn't like something someone said, I would reply, "whoever says it is it — you've got a cake-face." It's curious, because as an adult the sages taught me "Thou art That," which has practically the same effect. And philosophy tells us: "What

X says about Z tells us more about X than about Z." This made me sad when I found out she left me because she thought I was crazy.

Devoting oneself to reality is useless — what matters most is imagining what this place I'm in really is. Yet whether we devote ourselves to reality or fantasy, we're always devoting ourselves to something, and this seems to cost us. Besides, whenever we devote ourselves to one, the other appears on its own, in response.

Cloning makes me think about all the things they'll try to do. Fantasizing... at the beginning of these experiments, we might come to see, through some device, the soul leaving the body. Then, as the experiments progress, we'd wait for the soul of the dying, and induce it to enter a new body previously prepared and chosen by itself. If the experiments succeed, we would eventually not even need to wait for death — we could leave the unwanted body at will and enter one we've prepared. Later on, we wouldn't even need to prepare bodies anymore — we'd pass from one to another, even trade bodies, through the awareness gained in the initial experiences. And further still, though it would've been better not to go through all that, we'd discover that the subtle soul which glides from body to body can actually take on any form it wants, at any moment — we'd be able to shape ourselves however we wish, if we choose to live in a subtler world. And we'd discover too that the preparation of the dense body was really done naturally through the development of thought — and that anyone born into an unwanted body is so because their soul did nothing to beautify the world, which is how a new body is prepared. Even so, happiness is found in the unification of all forms, not in any one, no matter how subtle or beautiful. It is known that sages choose neutrality, not beauty. And the wisest of all wish for no body — they wish to be all bodies, God.

Nature deals with what is, in the moment it is, and with its raw reality at all times. What politics could we need for that? Whenever humans relate to nature through politics, they pollute it. The art of hypocrisy fills us with garbage. The best government is the one whose president nobody remembers, because a good administrator does not burden the people with excessive taxes or laws, nor annoy them with ambitions of becoming a heroic celebrity. A good government should be like God's: only 10 laws, 10% in taxes (if you want), and neither seen nor heard. No one can improve on that — and he actually gives us life.

We could program a computer with the basic functions of administration, and we'd eliminate human error, corruption, cronyism, monopolies, scams, double-talk, and all kinds of human flaws. For state projects and decisions we'd use popular vote as many times as necessary, including to reform the administrative program. Of course human judgment, experienced and compassionate, will always be necessary to decide. But with open information across the whole network, and the participation of most qualified individuals. The best part? The computer would be programmed never to declare war.

Why do we keep consuming things that should cost at least ten times less than we pay? Why do we accept paying more than something is worth just because demand inflated its value? Why do we keep selling cheaper to those who have more buying power, and not to those who need it most? Why do we talk about equality, while constantly selling privileges? Why do we speak of freedom while being burdened with more rules, laws, taxes, and permits? How is it possible that in today's Judeo-Christian societies, where the sacred book says a tithe is 10%, it has become 30 or even 70% to just survive? By 2050, will we be paying 90% taxes? And with all the laws and permits for control, we end up like communists — just a few producers tied to the state imposing their rules. What irony! These opposing ideologies ended up producing similar results, because they all believe in the illusion of control, authority, power, and money, and delight in their egos. But we all know what happens when a balloon inflates too much. Their hyperproduction model made them believe more work creates more wealth and jobs. But more production also led to more births, which doubled and tripled, and now there are more people without jobs to sustain. And those few who still produce something, not only manipulate and monopolize out of fear their neighbors will compete and steal profit — they also keep inventing machines to automate everything, so that no one but them works or earns. Who are they going to sell their goods to if no one works? Well, that might be the good part — in the end, everything will have to become free (but only if you obey, like slavery).

It seems that the greatest inventions of modern man are destroying the natural development of life and have turned people into slaves of their greedy, rapacious inventors — who conspired with politicians to orchestrate the great robbery known as "Patents." In the end, in the spiritual sense, one might say the Church was right to resist the advance of technology. But now, at last! Now we are truly free — to take the lives of millions with the push of a button! Thanks to our glorious technological achievements.

But nothing to fear, as long as everyone buys their machines and guns to kill each other and keep the economy flowing.

-Who are you?
-You! are who.
-Who am I?
-I! am who.

I've always lived among gods
and didn't realize it.

The "I" is a void moving from body to body. When it enters so-and-so, so-and-so says: I, from here, see that, see this, I like that. Then the void moves toward that thing, and that thing starts to speak from itself too. Sometimes it seems like there are many "I"s speaking at once — it's because the void can focus on however many bodies it wants. But it's always the same concentration of emptiness flowing through different forms. Sometimes it likes to jump from one to the next, creating conflict, delighting in the ignorance we're trapped in.

If she doesn't stare at you, dumbfounded and with a goofy look, she doesn't love you.

If you don't stare at her, dumbfounded and with a goofy look, you don't love her.

Fear is God desiring us.

To obtain what we want there is a need to concentrate on what we like is made of. But everything is made of God.

We live whirling around God.

- 2005 -

Happiness—a paradise on Earth we remember only in flashes, moments of ecstasy that shake our ground and leave our whole being hypnotizedly stunned. A contour that shines without light, an unforeseen wind that carries us away, a scent that lifts us off the ground, a gentle breath of tenderness impossible to hold; the entire quest of the human being, God's gift to His creation. How could we be so clumsy? How could we eat that apple? How could we believe we could be the creators of that fullness that surpasses us? How could we think that a society devoted to the triumph's demon preacher, could satisfy us more than God? How could we believe that by copying the images of that precious moment that once overwhelmed us, we would become happy gods? The original sin still drags us into attempting to build plenitude. Success (at the expense of others' failures), power (to manipulate others), fame (in need of others), riches (of a maniac dissatisfaction career), beautiful appearances (clinging to fleeting inequality); the desire for more and more... the God we betrayed. It would seem that

God likes our failure (of not knowing how to read between parentheses). He and all his messengers in the most varied ways recommended to us: Renunciation—an exemplary sacrifice for hopelessly confused children, who have not yet grasped the simple truth: that duty and passion are inseparable; that after duty comes what is wanted, and after what is wanted, comes duty once more.

Jesus Christ said of himself that he didn't do his will, what he wanted, but what his Father wanted, his duty. And he cried out in pain, begging us to forget ourselves.

Gautama Buddha also announced in the Diamond Sutra: "A Bodhisattva does not cling to the illusion of a separate individuality, or ego-entity identification. In truth, there is no 'self' to liberate, nor 'others' to be liberated... His love is infinite and cannot be limited by personal ties and ambitions... In fraud of illusion, all things are distinctly considered or attributed, but in the truth no differentiation is possible".

And the Prophet of Allāh has said: "You do not exist now, and existed before the creation of the world... You think you are, but you're not and never have existed... God is no different from you, and you do not differ from him; if by ignorance you think you are different from him, it means that you have an uneducated mind".

The enigmatic Lǎozǐ announced: "From nonbeing, we understand its essence, and from being, we see its appearance... Whoever practices non-action governs everything... Heaven and earth owe their durability at making themselves not the reason for its existence; so are eternal. The sage stays behind, thus he is ahead. Excludes himself and his person is preserved. Because it is selfless, gets its own sake".

The ineffable Kṛṣṇa: "The wise never seek delight in the things of this world, because the pleasures that they report are just a harbinger of coming suffering. Everything is transitory, as it comes, it goes... only if they have given up their will, they will reach the heights..."

In the most ancient Hindu texts: the sacred Upaniṣad; we find the answer of the Death, to the wise Nachiketā, when he scorn all earthly pleasures that were offered to him: "Although you've seen the satisfaction of all desires, the foundation of the world, the endless rewards of good deeds, the shore where there is no fear, lauded in all praise, and the great abode; have been wise and with firm determination you have despised all... If the one who kills believes that it is he who kills, and if the one who dies believes that it is he who dies, both not understand, because no one kills, nor the other is killed by anyone... The children run after external pleasures and fall into the trap that Death tends them. Only the wise, knowing the nature of what is immortal, seek nothing stable between all the unstable".

Even the majestic Sōkrátēs affirms in the Phaidōn: "Those among them who have sufficiently purified themselves through the practice of philosophy live forever without bodies, and go to dwell in even more beautiful abodes...".

So many religious recommendations that God sent to us in every language demonstrate that he really loves us in spite of our stubbornness.

So many sacred recommendations that God has sent us in every language show us that, despite our stubbornness, He truly loves us.

But why does it seem that God desires the failure of our will and our being? Or is it that we have so little faith we can't believe a better happiness exists than the one we just had—and we are consumed by anxiety and desperation at its loss, needing to chase it down and trap it in the prison of our possession, to summon it back like a puppet? Sometimes without realizing that once we manage to buy the toy, it loses its charm, and we become puppets ourselves to new, glittering illusions.

That is why renouncing ourselves must simply mean waiting—waiting and having faith that God will fill us with Himself just around the next corner. He said to us: "Ask and it shall be given." But the only thing we should ask for is Him, because the only thing that makes something bring us joy is that He is there, hidden behind the object that moves us, disguised, asking us to discover Him behind His images and likenesses; in all things, for the good of all, not just our own.

- 2007 -

Pride, fear, and greed made a pact and drew the borders. What can be done? You shouldn't argue too much with madmen—they only learn by crashing into the wall.

The government of the wise should be organized in such a way that its long-term goal is its own dissolution, since, after all, in nature everything dissolves eventually. But the dissolution of government must come only when the governed have learned to live without the harsh hand; when they no longer kill and rob one another—a situation far from our reality. Still, the ideal should not be discarded just for being an ideal. That's what ideals are for: to guide reality forward, even if we're light-years away from reaching it. The ideal seeks to teach people to live by themselves, free, less dependent on governance.

God gave us only ten laws, which hardly anyone respects—not even the Church at times—for they have spied, invaded, robbed, imprisoned, tortured, and killed in the name of God and freedom—a madness beyond compare. Some make the people kneel before their personal interests, which they call "laws," further impoverishing, controlling, and alienating them—turning them into slaves of the heroic theater of a manipulative machine. The great problem with power is that those who gain it start believing others should act as they think best for all. That is the beginning of legislating life—and legislating freedom (but only for others). Power goes to their heads—it's the most addictive drug.

Only two laws, said the Son of God, truly matter: Love God, and love others as yourself. And both are completely beyond human judgment, because no one can measure from the outside how much another loves God, others, or themselves. But we can say this: Everyone likes to live in freedom, without being told how to live their life. We like to be taught—but not indoctrinated.

That's why we must educate against the proud, the greedy, and the fearful—those who drown us in abusive rules and, in their ignorance, think it fair to do business with their citizens, finding ever more ways to take from them.

We must promote peace and reconciliation, and free ourselves from so many prohibitions, permits, and one-sided taxes. Which of these groups or institutions is the most perverse? Religion? Government? Military? Police? Corporations? Bankers? Politicians? Bureaucrats? Salesmen? Journalists? Aristocrats? Artists? Scientists? The masses of consumers? All of them, no doubt, were created with the best of intentions—but we must stay alert, because evil infiltrates any of them for its designs. Evil enters where there is success—it manipulates, divides, and destroys whatever it can. That is why no member of any institution should give too much power to its leaders. Power should be distributed as widely as possible. And we must know when to disobey—when leaders oppose common sense, when they promote harm and deprivation. No one should follow orders blindly; each one has their own conscience and is responsible for their actions.

We must think of the city of God: Paradise. Without borders, without governments, without institutions—a human being purely free in the knowledge and presence of God. Where people do not manipulate, rob, or kill each other; where peace has been conquered from within—not through force and weapons, but through the awareness of common sense and the mutual need for truth. Even if it's utopian, we should begin thinking this way—little by little, step by step. Let us not discard the idea just because it can't be realized right away.

To begin with, people of such nature would have only one desire: God—fullness, happiness. For discord belongs only to those who desire worldly objects and fight over them. So then, as a society, what is it that we advertise? Are we really capable of entering this paradise of peace? Or would we kill to save or sell our objects? "Whoever wants to save their life will lose it," said the Son of God. But our entire modern culture stinks of colored mirrors and largely promotes the opposite.

First of all, competition is never healthy—only mutual cooperation is. Pride, promoted as the ideal feeling to follow, is the seed of evil. And lying just to sell—which feels so natural—is like sinking into quicksand. The more gold we hold in our hands, the more heavily we sink. You cannot fly high with that much weight in your pockets.

Second: Governments are not the parents of citizens, nor chosen superior beings. They are merely employees of the people, hired to do a simple administrative task. But the citizen is also corrupt, and when given even a little power, abuses the weak and mistreats them. Thus, business-owning citizens are tightfisted and make life hard and strict for their workers. Were it not for the government, they would enslave them. And they don't treat their clients much better—constantly tricking them to take as much as possible. They pay the lowest wages, dress employees in full corporate gear, and make them run like machines—just to wave the flag of their hypocrisy. The workers grow bitter, forced to wear fake smiles and pretend they're all friends. And the worst part is—even aware of all this, many people submit and even buy from those same exploiters. To make matters worse, they sell more to those who have more—they grow richer by selling cheaper to big buyers—when logic says: to balance any scale, we must give more to those who have less.

Third—and this really takes the cake—so many universities have only served to make us need more and more products to survive, all protected by exclusive rights so no one can copy them or benefit from them. But the opposite should be encouraged—people should be motivated to copy everything, to make it themselves, to get all the benefit they can. Only this is true freedom, and true evolution for all.

And fourth, to end on a cordial note: Let us stop paying ridiculous sums of money for spectacles and flashy distractions. Instead of watching so many clowns, we should try to understand something about this world.

- 2008 -

I still read modern philosophers asking themselves questions like these: What is a successful life? How can one feel satisfied with their life? What is life for?

Surely it isn't for having a child, planting a tree, writing a book, becoming a winner, or making a lot of money—despite the collective imagination of our society. Because bringing a child into this world of suffering is more irresponsible than meritorious; and planting a tree shouldn't even be necessary if we lived according to nature. Many people have written books, yet their lives don't serve as examples; and to be a winner in one thing you must lose in many others—not to mention being willing to make someone else the loser. And money and power only make us addicted and end up bringing out the worst in us.

So then maybe life is about fulfilling our desires—chasing after silly, fleeting pleasures while we can, even if we don't know how this existence of ours came to be, or what lies beyond death. That doesn't seem like a good option, and though it's the most common and natural one, we always grow tired of our toys in the end. Which is why even if we conquered the whole world, we would still be as fickle, stubborn, and ignorant as before. There's no fulfillment in force—using force to convince is always painful and creates enemies. Not to mention that all that force will be theirs when the world turns around.

Dedicating oneself exclusively to something and doing it with perfection seems like nothing more than wasted concentration on something transiently absurd. Even if the greatest works come from such dedication, that doesn't make it the purpose of life.

Protecting, caring for, and feeding others sounds like a noble life, and we'd have to take off our hats to it. But even if we healed them of all their illnesses, they might never abandon their sinful tendencies. And even though we are protected by those who have received our care, we have not achieved any goal by simply being healthy.

Searching for truth and studying seems like the best option. Studying this very life in any of its aspects is the seed of evolution, since study brings the reward of discovery. Searching and discovering new horizons, exploring and experimenting makes us adventurous and free, and allows us to always get something new out of life. This is much closer—but it still depends on the intention. Humanity's discoveries have made us completely dependent on the artificial, and we haven't transcended our nature at all. These discoveries are now used to do harm and become a burden for others. Knowing how something works, accessing its mechanisms, and manipulating them does not fulfill life.

People used to be born with the duty of hunting or farming to eat. Now they're born with the duty to have an ID, money, a refrigerator, a phone, a car, to graduate from multiple schools, and if they're lucky, to spend eight hours under the command of other fools almost every day of their lives. They can't even build their homes the way they want—they must be inspected and pay a juicy permit. On top of that, they have to pay for their future—and they call this "insurance." And not only that, they also have to pay to work: anything they want to sell will only be possible if they pay another hefty fee. They can't even imitate the more clever neighbor's way of surviving, because he's protected by copyright and can sue them.

And since they've become so proudly careless, "they're forced" to wear seatbelts, to not do drugs, and to behave in public. We're now surrounded by technologies that make us more dependent, more polluted, and more impoverished. How successful can we say these discoveries really are? What we can say is that man is increasingly enslaved by his own sins.

What's left after all these frustrated, ignorant attempts at life? A successful life is one that has learned to love God above all things and whose only desire is to merge into Him. Any of the actions we mentioned earlier can bring complete satisfaction if done for the joy of doing it for all, for God. For that moment of gratitude toward the One who gave us the ability to act and create joy, life is redeemed. And since we want God to accept us, we must accept others—not despise or harm them, no matter how negligent they may seem—for they are there to constantly remind us of our own negligence and ignorance before the universe, before God.

God created this world with the most peaceful of intentions.

I imagine He must have said: "So that creatures do not compete, fight, or kill one another for Me, the only true goal and happiness, I will make it so that only those who have nothing, or have lost everything, may reach Me."

Did God imagine that His creatures would turn out to be so jealous of one another, that they would end up competing anyway? That instead of collaborating, they would hide from one another, lie, steal, and even kill for fleeting things of no real value to our existence? And still feel proud and superior because of it.

- 2010 -

To see things the way we see them, all it takes is a certain kind of ignorance. Or, put another way: we are merely a certain ignorance filtering reality, making us see things as we do.

When an idea circles around something, concentration begins. It gathers energy, and when that energy is released, it produces an effect—a reaction of that something to our persistent circling.

- 2012 -

It's not that pursuing goodness is wrong. It's that there is no "good" to be pursued for the happiness that is everywhere. Happiness does not reject evil—it is evil that refuses to be happy in that way, that rejects reality, rejects God, and draws away from Him in a kind of suicide. That is why we must imitate God in this: always try to heal the wicked and help them find joy. But with the understanding that such joy can never come from our own hands, only from God.

I thought it didn't need to be said, but from our point of view, everyone has a god. For those who claim not to believe in God, their god is "No"—the negation of everything, until they even deny themselves and the act of denial. Some make gods of themselves, or of their will to power, or their will to choose. Others make a god of an experience and call it Tao, Nirvana, Logos, or Holy Spirit. Some turn it into unity, but then give it a specific name and differentiate it from the rest. The most amusing ones turn whatever they can hold in their hands into god, and spend their lives collecting little yellow or transparent stones. All of these are gods too—great ideas, great spirits. But the true God is one within them all.

bibliography

I Ching - Book of changes	2000 bc
Upanishads	1000 bc
The Iliad and the Odyssey – *Homer*	760 bc
Torah	580 bc
Tao Te King - *Lao Tse*	550 bc
The Diamond Sutra and others – (*Buddha* teachings)	500 bc
Dialogues and others – *Plato*	390 bc
Chuang Tzu – *Zhuangzi*	350 bc
Bhagavad Gita	200 bc
The Bible of Jerusalem – New Testament	100
The Tibetan Book of the Dead - *Padmasambhava*	800
Unity Treaty – *Ibn 'Arabi*	1200
Summa Theologica – *St. Thomas Aquinas*	1265
Treatises and Sermons - *Meister Eckhart*	1300
The Prince – *Machiavelli*	1513
Ethics - *Baruch de Spinoza*	1677
Theory of Nature, Faust and others - *W. Von Goethe*	1832
Walden and others - *Henry David Thoreau*	1854
Rhymes and Legends - *G. A. Bécquer*	1870
Thus Spoke Zarathustra and others - *Friedrich Nietzsche*	1891
Course in General Linguistics - *Ferdinand de Saussure*	1913
The Divine Life - *Sri Aurobindo*	1914
In Search of Lost Time - *Marcel Proust*	1922
Essays in Zen Buddhism - *D. T. Suzuki*	1927
Everything and Nothing - *Macedonio Fernández*	1972
The Tao of Physics - *Fritjof Capra*	1975
Synergetics - *Hermann Haken*	1981
Goodbye to Philosophy and other texts - *E. M. Cioran*	1991
The Vision of Rishis - *Swami Dayananda*	1995

The data of the years of the thinkers, is an approximation with the sole intention of creating a reference time line.

www.ingramcontent.com/pod-product-compliance
Lightning Source LLC
Chambersburg PA
CBHW070303010526
44108CB00039B/1698